ANNIE OAKLEY

Annie Oakley at the height of her career, wearing the more conspicuous of the many medals presented to her by famous societies, celebrities, and members of royalty.

ANNIE OAKLEY
WOMAN AT ARMS

A Biography By

COURTNEY RYLEY COOPER

KONECKY&KONECKY

KONECKY & KONECKY
150 FIFTH AVE.
NEW YORK, NY 10011

ISBN: 1-56852-271-1

LIST OF PLATES

DRAWINGS IN TEXT

ANNIE OAKLEY

Chapter One

IN the autumn of 1926, they laid away "Little Missy's" sewing basket, her fine needles, the unfinished pieces of embroidery which, dainty stitch after dainty stitch, had grown under her skilled fingers and sharp eyes from the embryo of a mere stamped pattern to works of artistry. But some of these were brought forth again; there were those grateful for even a bit of uncompleted fancy work, if that trifle of linen and floss could form an intrinsic remembrance of a white haired woman who in all her life had done naught but kindness, who had given of her store of wealth that suffering might be alleviated, the uneducated benefited by the advantage of books and schooling, generosity provided where penury had been before; the "Little Missy" had first-hand knowledge of what hardships meant, and even the adulation of millions who once used her name more frequently than that of the ruling President of the United States could not wipe out a feeling of comraderie for all whose

lot might not be of the happiest. A philanthro-
pist? Not at all, in the common acceptation of
the term. She perhaps would have resented the
word. Such things were merely the outpouring
of the nature of a woman who had fought her
way from virtual slavery to a position, in which,
for a span of years at least, she was the most
famous feminine personage in the entire world.
Her name was Mrs. Frank E. Butler. If that
means nothing, reflect then upon the more magi-
cal one of Annie Oakley.

The world moves swiftly enough that the
heroine of one generation may be, to a certain
degree at least, forgotten in the next. So was it
with Annie Oakley in the broad sense; there is
at hand a clipping from a news syndicate written
a few months before her death by Will Rogers,
which emphasizes this phase of things rather
acutely. It is in far different style from the
comedian's daily quips; a touch of sentiment instead of the usual jest:

"This is a good story about a little woman that
all the older generation remember. She was the
reigning sensation of America and Europe during
the heyday of Buffalo Bill's Wild West show. She
was their star. Her picture was on more billboards
than a modern Gloria Swanson. It was Annie Oakley, the greatest woman rifle shot the world has ever

4.

produced. Nobody took her place. There was only one. She is bedridden from an automobile accident a few years ago. She for years taught the fashionable people at Pinehurst, N. C., to shoot. America is worshipping at the feet of Raquel Meller, the Spanish lady. Europe talked the same of Annie Oakley in her day. I want you to write her, all you who remember her, and those that can go and see her. Her address is 706 Lexington Avenue, Dayton, Ohio. She will be a lesson to you. She is a greater character than she was a rifle shot. Circuses have produced the cleanest living class of people in America today, and Annie Oakley's name, her lovable traits, her thoughtful consideration of others, will live as a mark for any woman to shoot at."

In a pile of letters, clippings and old pictures, I found the answer to the tribute of Will Rogers as I compiled the material for this book. Annie Oakley gave up her fight for life a few months after the squib concerning her appeared. In the effects which remained to be culled over by a biographer, were packet upon packet of letters, from every part of the world, which had gone forward to her in response to the appeal of the cowboy comedian. Most of these were genuine tributes, from persons who had known her in other days, from men and women who remembered the greatest thrill of childhood, that day in fact, when the Wild West Show had come to town and they had formed a part of the big audience which had gathered to witness the stalwart Buffalo Bill introduce his Congress of Rough Riders of the World, and see Annie Oakley, "Little Sure Shot" as the Indian warrior, Sitting Bull, had called her, perform the feats of marksmanship which had made her name world-wide. Others were from persons who had heard of her and never seen her, genuine epistles of cheer and of sympathy. Then there was a type which was entirely different.

These were from individuals who never forget self. In writing with the ostensible idea of cheering one who fought against the idleness of incapacity, particularly galling to one who ever has known activity and the outdoors, they had accomplished that "cheering" process by dilating upon their own troubles. Still others had hinted at monetary misfortunes. And more had been perfectly frank in their statement that they wished Miss Annie Oakley every happiness, and would Miss Oakley please remember that there were others in the world who were unfortunate, especially the writer? Any amount, no matter how small—or large—would be appreciated by return mail. This biographer procured quite an insight into the true nature of the woman the world knew as Annie Oakley as a result of those letters; not from the epistles themselves, it is true. It came from a single word, written by a hand now still, across the face of each begging epistle:

"Answered."

How much money those answers contained is a matter which Annie Oakley knew and no one else. That was one of her habits. Someway, it was remindful of another figure of prominence in the days when Annie Oakley's name was a matter of great import.

One rainy night, Colonel William Frederick Cody, (Buffalo Bill) and myself were walking across the soggy circus lot of a little town in Texas. Times and conditions had changed for Buffalo Bill. No longer was he the head of the organization which he had known when Annie Oakley was his feminine star, and such persons as Queen Victoria sent personal messages to the tents of the two exponents of the West with a request for a private audience. No longer were the riches pouring in; the lean, sinewy hands which had felt the touch of millions now clasped but comparatively few dollars; debts and bad investments, well intentioned plans come to naught, avaricious hangers-on, friends in name only,—these agencies had wilted the

Cody fortunes, and he was at the present time barely providing himself with an existence; at least, there was only an existence left after the bills, the attachments, the debt-collectors and others had been taken care of on pay day. A changed Buffalo Bill in his financial status; the same old Buffalo Bill, however, of heyday times as concerned his geniality, his love of the West, his child-like faith that he would remain always strong and stalwart, able to mount a horse on the fly, and retain his shooting accuracy forever. And the same old Buffalo Bill in still another respect.

The show was over. In the glare of the calciums the tents were dropping; tired, struggling horses floundered through the mud as they hauled the wagons to the loading runs for the journey to the next town. Here and there, shadowy, vague, in the misty light, the "pick-up" crew moved about the lot; there is always extra caution on a rainy night that every item of paraphernalia be catalogued, every movement checked, to guard against valuable perquisites being left behind. One of these checkers-up, we believed, stood in our path. But as we came nearer, we saw that he wore a blue coat, and thumbed a G. A. R. tri-color of red, white and blue in a button-hole.

8.

Buffalo Bill bent low as the man mumbled a sentence. Then a big hand went into a pocket and fumbled there. A queer light came into Buffalo Bill's eyes, then passed. He handed the applicant a dollar and we walked on.

We reached the main street, there to part for the night, I to go to my hotel, Buffalo Bill to go to his car on the railroad train. A taxi appeared, and I hailed it, for the Colonel. But as the door opened, the plainsman hesitated and drew back.

"Badlands," he said—a nickname he had bestowed years before—"there's just one thing that stands between me and this taxi."

"What's that, Colonel?"

Buffalo Bill laughed and put forth a hand.

"Oh stop asking questions," he boomed, "and lend me a dollar 'till pay day!"

It was not unusual that either Buffalo Bill or Annie Oakley should know how to give. The story of Cody's youth has been told many times, of the boy who filled the role of a man with the bull-whacking outfits then traveling what then was known as the Great American Desert, that he might, at the end of a dangerous trip, pour his earnings into the lap of a mother for whom he formed the sole support, his killing of his first Indian at the age of eleven, his main schooling gained as he lay starving in a dugout, unable to move because of a broken leg, while his companion fought the drifts of a blizzard through a hundred miles of wilderness in an effort to aid his comrade. Few know Annie Oakley's story, yet it is one which pales even that of Buffalo Bill; one expects heroism from a strong, western boy. The heroism of Annie Oakley, however, is almost of the fiction type; it goes even beyond that, for fiction, for the main part, must, at least, be probable.

One finds difficulties in discovering a counterpart for the woman known as Annie Oakley, for there are none that arise easily to hand in the feminine world. Hardships were her lot, of the most terrible character; yet one finds her memory of those hardships subdued in something greater; the clarity of blue skies, the whirr of the partridge in the brush, the moonlight upon the bivouacked fields of garnered corn. When Annie Oakley spoke of her childhood, it was these things which were paramount; she could forget the unpleasantries when these memories arose.

Yet unpleasantries they were, of a type which would cause the ordinary mind to become a bitter, morose, beaten thing; even before the advent of Phoebe Anna Oakley Mozee, there had been a background of suffering, which, in the telling, describes rather vividly the changes, both economic and social, which have come to America within the last century. Today, such a set of circumstances would be thoroughly out of the ordinary; but at the time of the marriage of Annie Oakley's mother, there were no such agencies as humane officers, juvenile courts, settlement investigators and others whom, at times, we are prone to look upon as somewhat of a bore, but who need only such instances as that of the woman who bore Annie Oakley—as well as Annie Oakley herself—to justify their existence.

It was in 1847 that a Quaker hotel keeper named Jake Mozee, turned from the road toward a ramshackle farmhouse in a small valley near Hollidaysburg, Pa., in answer to the sound of a weeping child. Investigating, he at last found a girl of twelve, hiding beneath a stairway; and raising her in his arms, the man questioned her regarding her tears.

Her name was Susanne, the girl said. Her mother had died some years before, to be followed by a stepmother. Then her father had passed away, and the stepmother had in turn married again, thus making the girl a stepchild in a double sense. Two other sisters, resenting the treatment of alien parents, had left home,

leaving this child and a baby to bear the brunt of
a lack of affection. The girl told of cruelties,
and the hotel keeper—Jake Mozee was about
twenty years her senior—went forth in search of
the stepfather.

He found the man in the field and obtained
from him a promise that he would treat the
child with more affection in the future. However, a short time later, in passing the house, he
again discovered the child in tears, and resorted
to an action that, in these times, would, at least
be called hasty.

There was no further remonstrance with
either stepmother or stepfather. Jake Mozee
simply led the child to the gate where his horse
was hitched, mounted, pulled the girl to a position behind him, told her to "hold on," dug his
spurs into his mount and departed. Today, such
an event might be called kidnapping. But in
the days when Annie Oakley's mother was a
girl—in the remote districts at least—it merely
seemed to be a fortuitous happening with no
subsequent action of law or even of personal
remonstrance.

During the later years of her lifetime, Annie
Oakley put into the form of a story, or rather,
scattered notes, the events of her lifetime, with
particular stress upon the earlier years. The

event of a Pennsylvania Lochinvar who rode from his hotel and carried away a twelve year old bride-to-be elicited little more comment than the recital of the facts themselves. What became of the stepfather or stepmother seemed to be of little consequence. As far as can be gleaned from the notes, they merely stood in the doorway, watched their unwelcome stepchild carried away—then returned to the more important things of life.

As for the child, her rescuer placed her for a few years in the care of a sister who lived some distance from his little hotel. However, the tempestuous beginning of their acquaintance-ship was to have equally tempestuous sequences. When the girl was about fifteen years of age, and Jake Mozee consequently about thirty-five, he rode one day to see her. He asked her to marry him. She assented; according to Annie Oakley's diary, that was the extent of their courtship.

Life began now in the little hotel where it continued for three years, during which time, two children, both girls, were born. Then one night ten days after the birth of the second child and while the mother, then only about eighteen years of age, was still ill as a result, a hotel guest, reading late, upset a kerosene lamp. Jake Mozee

rescued his wife and babies. There was no insurance; it was not a favorable investment in
those days. Banking suffered from the same contumely; many of the banking houses were private affairs, no more staple than the persons who
owned them; the wise person hoarded his money
in a secret hiding place, believing it safer to risk
the danger of robbery or of fire than the more
certain loss by dishonesty of a trustee or mis-
management. The hotel had been the Mozee
bank. When that hotel had become embers, the
same fate had befallen every saving.

It meant a new beginning and for several
years Mozee strove to rehabilitate himself in his
old surroundings. Little came to him except
another daughter; finally, with the lure of new
land and new beginnings before them, the family
obtained the money for a railroad journey into
what was then a sparsely settled district of Ohio,
proceeding from Greenville, where they left the
railroad, thirty miles inland to Darke County,
through swamps and over corduroy roads to a
spot near a tiny, cross-roads settlement known as
Woodland. Here began a new fight for existence upon a leased tract of land, where, in a
tiny hewn cabin, nothing seemed to prosper save
a constantly augmented family of girls. Three
were born within almost as many years, the last

of whom was Phoebe Anne Oakley Mozee. Two
more years brought a boy, making now a family

*The cabin at Woodland, Darke County, Ohio, where Annie
Oakley was born, August 13th, 1866.*

of six, one of the girls having died. Another,
Emily, was to swell the total to seven.

It was strictly a pioneer household. Clothing
was of homespun, the shoes for the "stair-step"

brood of children cut from the hide of the first
young beef, butchered with the coming of the
first "cold-snap." Life was a thing of conserva-
tion in those days; the smoking of the hams and
shoulders of home butchered hogs over a constantly smouldering pile of hickory chips, the
pickling of beans and cucumbers, the preserving
of fruits and the drying of apples, peaches and
pears was intermingled with the garnering of
vegetables and "putting them down" in dry
straw beneath a heavy covering of turf to protect them against frost in the preparation for the
winter when the fruits of summer toil must provide when no other food was procurable. The
store, as such, played but a small part in the life
of the average farmer in such districts as that
which, even sixty years or seventy ago, formed
to a certain extent a pioneering district of
America. One likes to think of the pioneer as a
person wandering the untrammelled districts of
the West, and to a large degree, that is of course
true. But the thing which made Western
pioneers the hardy, venturesome persons that
they were was the fact that they had in a great
many instances already been pioneers in what
now is called the over-populated areas of the
East. Many a forty-niner, making his stake in
California, found living conditions but little

worse than those he had known, back on the
worm-fenced, scrabble-soiled farm of what now
is termed, at the farthest, the Middle West.

So it was with Jake Mozee, his wife and his
brood. The one big event of the year, in fact,
was when the father, excited over the long trip,
took his summer store of wheat and corn to the
mill, fourteen miles away, returning with the
store luxuries needed for the winter—rice and
sugar and coffee. Upon such a journey, Jake
Mozee started at daybreak one autumn morning
about four years after Annie Oakley's birth.
There had been excessive rain-storms; the
poorly made roads were in many places little
more than bog-holes, and to this was added the
threat of another onslaught of inclement
weather.

It arrived before Mozee had well begun his
journey to the mill—one of those sudden de-
scents which so often come after a stretch of
rainy weather in the mid-eastern autumn; a
quick fall of temperature, a sudden sweeping of
the wind, carrying upon its breast a mist which
froze as it fell, and converting the world to
glass. Soon the snow began, resolving itself
swiftly into the howling fierceness of a blizzard.
Mozee reached the mill after a terrific struggle.
Leaving his grain, he proceeded then to the pur-

chase of his groceries at the cross-roads store, returning to the mill for his flour, meal, "shorts"
and bran, the necessities of a winter sojourn
away from civilization. The storm had become
worse now, against the advice of the mill-keeper
he set forth; he had told his family he would return: they would be "waitin' up" for him, and,
a blurred figure in the driving white, he began
the journey home.

In Annie Oakley's notes is a short passage
which tells:

"That night, my mother kept big logs blazing in
the fireplace until the light shone brightly through
the windows and penetrated the darkness beyond.
The supper table, with its simple evening meal, was
left untouched, except that we smaller children had
eaten our 'ponade', consisting of home-made bread,
cut into small squares, boiling water slightly flavored
with brandy, some maple sugar and the whole
covered by cream.

"As the night progressed, Mother became more
nervous. Small as I was, I can remember her face
as she knelt and prayed for Daddy's return. Eleven
o'clock came; twelve o'clock, and then a wagon was
heard. My mother, thanking God between white
lips, threw open the door and ran forth into the
face of the raging storm. Daddy, with the reins
around his neck and wrists, for his hands were
frozen, sat upright in the seat of the wagon. He
did not answer my mother's greeting; speech was

gone. The horses had found their way through the open gate, come to the door, then stopped. They were steaming; the sweat was dripping from them. An armchair with a blanket over it was quickly taken to the side of the wagon; Daddy was extricated from the reins, then lifted down and carried within to the fireplace, but he had reached aid too late. He never walked again. The next March gave me a child-hood picture of my first grave, in the little cemetery two miles distant—a grave and a wooden headboard with the name of my father upon it."

That storm, which robbed Annie Oakley of her father seemed cruel at the time. But it carried an aftermath—it formed the beginning of a career which was to make her the most widely known woman of her generation.

Chapter Two

PERHAPS, some day, there may be a desire upon the part of some outdoor feminine organization, such as is exemplified in the Campfire Girls and others of this type, for a pattern by which to model, such as is supplied the Boy Scouts of America in the historic figures of Buffalo Bill and of Kit Carson. Certainly there are qualities in the story of Annie Oakley which should qualify her for such an exaltation, not only for what she did as a child, and what she accomplished as a woman to advance the fact—rather frowned upon in her time—that the feminine has as much right to surpass as the male, but for the cheeriness with which it all left her, the genuine sweetness, the clarity, both of thought and of action, the lack of bitterness, of egotism for things accomplished, of the flightiness which might have led to an entirely different sort of a name for a woman as feted and as widely known as Annie Oakley.

In the notes left by the greatest woman rifle shot, are many pertaining to her childhood and the causes which underlay her expertness with

20.

firearms. But when one reads those notes, one finds a singular lack of information concerning the difficulties which literally forced her into a position of exhibition fame; rather there is the constant dwelling upon the love of her childhood, the joy of home, the congeniality of sister and brother.

No doubt her home was happy, as far as mother love was concerned, the companionship of a brother who evidently adored her because of her tomboyish proclivities, and the love of sisters who, while they might not quite understand her, regarded her with no less affection. But from a standpoint of outside happenings, the existence of the child was anything but joyous.

It was a poor family which Jake Mozee left when he died as the result of his gruelling experience in the blizzard. The day after the lonely funeral the mother gathered her main possessions, which were the children, her few household effects and what money had been saved in the hiding place beneath the rafters of the little log home, and moved to a smaller place four miles away, which she procured upon a cash lease.

Some of the children were old enough to help her materially, others, such as Annie, could give but small aid, and the remainder were more of a burden than a blessing. But between them all, they someway managed to exist, and there came the time when the mother left the older daughters behind when she went to the field, that they might nurse a sister Mary, who had become afflicted with tuberculosis. The children worked in self-appointed shifts, watching beside their sister day and night. It was useless; death came in the spring, and death, to an already stricken family, far in the recesses of what was then pioneer country, meant far more than is usually encompassed by the term. The one cow was sold to aid with the payment of funeral and physician's expenses, the family then depending upon the precarious business of milking "Old Black," a half-wild bovine which had selected the Mozee place as a sort of headquarters, and which, to use Annie Oakley's own description, could best be forced to part with her provender by an approach with a pitchfork in one hand as a weapon of defense and a milk-pail in the other. Wild cows, wild hogs and boars, and other once domestic stock gone to the primitive, were not unusual in this district. An order of the Mozee household was that the children should venture alone no farther than the orchard fence because of the danger of wolves, gathering to gnaw at the bones of a beef animal which had died a short time previous.

The death of Mary brought stark poverty to the household. In fact, the straits became such that the last of the bread and bacon had been consumed and the family was largely existing upon what milk Old Black was willing to dispense, when faraway neighbors arrived with hams, a barrel of potatoes and other riches to aid a stricken mother and her brood to exist until summer. But in her notes, Annie Oakley brushed this but lightly. Far better to describe, when the day's work was done, how a worn young mother, taking new strength in her task, would erase the marks of a day's endeavors from her children, and then at even-tide, with her stair-steps clustered about her, sing the evening hymns.

As the years passed, and fortunes grew but little better, the tomboy of the family, now old enough to wander at will, betook herself more and more to the woods which abounded about the place. Game was plentiful: quail, rabbits, squirrel, and ruffed-grouse. Barely six years old, Annie—the more stilted name of Anne had never been used—appeared one evening with a dead quail in each hand, to brighten the larder. Where she had learned it, she does not reveal, but with a cunning that was at least precocious, she had sought out the haunts of the game-birds and there with heavy corn-stalks, built like a log-house and fastened with strings, had fashioned a crude trap, into which a trench ran, moving sharply upward, once it had gone under the little house of corn-stalks. This had been baited with grains of corn, leading to more within the trap, which had been covered with brush and twigs to remove it from the observation of the ever present foxes. These traps Annie Oakley visited each day; it was not long before the work of the child in this direction had taken an atmosphere of extreme importance in the life of the Mozee family. She was the provider of fresh meat, a delicacy where sow-belly or smoked beef proved the usual round of fare. This continued for a year or more, while constantly the eyes of the tomboyish Annie roved to a tremendous 40 inch cap and ball Kentucky rifle which hung over the fireplace and which had been one of the possessions lugged into the country when Jake Mozee and his girl wife had emigrated from Pennsylvania.

There was an air of mystery about that rifle. Being Quakers, with the Quaker prejudice against firearms of any sort, both Jake Mozee and his wife had regarded the gun as a thing to be used only in case of dire extremity; the journey had been a long one when they had left Pennsylvania for the far off country of Ohio, there had been weird stories of Indians, of ferocious animals, of physical dangers that would beset one who strove to build a home in a wilderness. Hence, in a moment of preparation, the rifle had been purchased, but with the first evidence of a lack of need from a standpoint of protection, it had been relegated to its hooks above the fireplace, to rust out its life, its loaded powder horn and caps and balls gathering dust nearby. There it formed a constant temptation to a child who already had grown to gain more than the ordinary thrill from the out-of-doors, and at last the enthrallment grew too great. She enlisted the aid of her brother, and went into conference. That evening, the rifle reposed again above the fireplace. The younger brother wore an air of deep secrecy, while Annie, the tomboy of the Mozee family, wore, in addition to an exceedingly satisfied expression, a nose which was red and bulbous, resultant from the kick of an overload. Mrs. Mozee paused in her evening work of "tidying up" the fireplace.

"Annie," she said, fastening upon her daughter one of those boring glances which only a mother can assume, "the next time thee feel thee must have the gun, ask me to help thee and thee'll not spill so much powder."

It was the beginning of a rifle career that was soon, however, to be halted. Before there had been many excursions afield, in which time however, the child learned to fire the old weapon without endangering her entire facial makeup, an interruption arrived in a short trip to town taken by Mrs. Mozee and a young man who had been paying frequent calls of late, Daniel Brumbaugh, a relative of "the" Brumbaughs of Pennsylvania. When the mother returned, it was with the information that the household possessed a new guardian and that the family would move again, this time to a place near the town of Greenville, where Brumbaugh had his business.

There is nothing to indicate that Brumbaugh was not a kind and worthy stepfather; as for Annie Oakley, she had but slight chance to know him whatever. A friend of the mother, a Mrs. Crawford Edington, who lived some distance from the Brumbaugh household, and whose husband was the superintendent of the County Infirmary, came to visit, and, perchance, seeing an opportunity to aid a family which presented more children than other forms of wealth, took Annie home for what was to have been a stay of only a few weeks.

26.

It lengthened however, into the winter, with the suggestion of Mrs. Edington that the child remain and attend school with her son, one year Annie's junior. It was a tremendous opportunity; school had been sadly lacking so far in the life of Annie Oakley.

This was a condition existent for many children who lived on out-of-the-way farms in the days just preceding and after the Civil War. But what they lacked in mental acceleration, they provided in agility of finger; the carding and weaving of wool, and needlework in all its phases were a part of the equipment of many a child who knew but little of readin', writin' or 'rithmetic. Annie Oakley had early shown an adeptness; now, at nine, she was more able than many women.

There was need for her skill. The Infirmary, from what hints are given in Annie Oakley's notes, was of a type not above its time, save for the constant work of the superintendent and his wife, striving to elevate a place where the orphan, the infirm, the beggar, the worthwhile poor, the good, the bad and the indifferent were sent with little regard for differentiation as long as they were a charge upon the county. Appropriations were few and far between; the salary of Edington was small, but much of this store went back to the infirmary that the condition of the county charges might be slightly bettered, while the wife gave what aid she could by the purchase or making of cloth, and the sewing of clothing, particularly for children. With this Annie assisted, but it all was gratuitous work, and her efforts counted for nothing in the Edington fortunes. There came the time when the superintendent's wife felt that she could not longer keep the child, and against her will, for a genuine love had arisen between the two, prepared for her homeward journey. A journey, however, that was not to be.

Mrs. Edington longed for advantages for the child. She dreamed of the day when she would become rich, and when she could send this bright-featured, alert girl, her head already massing with a wealth of chestnut hair, to fashionable schools, give her the advantages which her brain seemed to demand, and clothe her as an aristocratic appearing little being, pert and proud of bearing, deserved. One day, as if in answer to her dreams, a man whose horses and bright buggy, his clothing and general demeanor gave evidence of something more than penury, drove to the house with the plea that he be allowed to "take out" a girl from the infirmary to act as a companion for his wife and care for their young baby.

This was not an unusual condition a generation or more ago. The present day attitude toward orphans had not come into being; that a child was without parents or someone to care for it seemed to automatically remove what rights it might possess to judge or choose its own future. Children were farmed out from infirmaries with but scant regard for what might come to them as a result of it; the promise of the man or woman who took them away that they would be well cared for often was the sole assurance that the child would be treated with kindliness. There was no system of inspection, no reports, often no means of knowing the child's fate, once it had departed from the guardianship of the institution.

Inasmuch as Annie had formed a sort of lieutenant for Mrs. Edington during her winter's stay, she was proffered as a guide, while the busy superintendent's wife went on with her myriad duties. With the man in tow, the girl went to the infirmary while, like a buyer selecting stock, he looked over the offerings of unfortunate girls, the childish Annie Oakley, with a great feeling of importance, rattling on beside him as she told their qualities for good or bad. One after

another, the list was gone through, but the visitor
had, during his association with his diminuitive
guide, gained some unalterable ideas.   He
couldn't make up his mind, he said, and they
went back to the superintendent's house.

Who the man was, who his wife was, this
writer does not know.   Neither in conversation,
in letters or in her notes, did Annie Oakley seem
inclined to mention their true names.   She had
one of her own for them—it was that of The
Wolves.

A melodramatic title, it is true, but they evidently were melodramatic people with a melodramatic fate awaiting the child whom they
should take into their home.   The dinner table
conversation finally veered to that subject;
Annie Oakley had talked of her love of the open
country, of the woods, of the joy of the hunt, of
the thrill of trailing some animal to its natural
run that she might there set a trap for it.   And
as she talked, the jaws of a trap closed for her
also.

For the visitor began then to talk of his home
—a paradise of game, a tremendous farm, where,
if Annie chose, she could live a life of comparative ease, except of course, for the tasks of her
schooling; he must insist, said the visitor, that
the child he took should prepare her brain for

the future. In plain vernacular, he was an oily talker, playing upon unsophisticated folk.

The thought of a great farm she could roam as her own appealed to Annie Oakley. The dream of better things for a child whom she loved caught the fancy of Mrs. Edington. The man had said that none but Annie could fill the niche of love and kindness which existed in a distant farmhouse. The conversation finally took on a definite tone with the decision that Mrs. Edington would write to Annie's mother, urging her that she give her child this golden opportunity.

Two weeks later, the visitor returned, to find that the mother's answer had been consent. Joyously, a nine year old girl set forth into the world with a total stranger, trusting to his story of happiness. But it wasn't true.

The mere task of caring for their baby resolved itself into something far different. Instead, she was awakened at four o'clock, to hurry forth to the milking of two cows, the feeding of them, of the pigs and chickens and of the calves, after which she prepared breakfast, washed the dishes, pumped fresh water into the trough for the cattle, rocked the baby to sleep, weeded the garden, picked wild blackberries, attended to the sweeping and cleaning about the house, and then, these chores done, rushed to the

31.

ANNIE OAKLEY

preparation of luncheon—it was called dinner
then, and was a man's sized meal—which must
be hot and steaming upon the table by 11.30
o'clock. Again were there dishes to wash, again
chores, and hardly were they done before milking time came again and the necessity for preparing "supper." It was a tired, disillusioned
Annie Oakley who dragged her way to the
gaunt, illy-furnished room under the rafters,
ghostly appearing in the flickering light of the
one candle, when her work was done.

The family lived like pigs. Instead of a bedroom, there was a curtained off partition at one
end of the living room where the man and his
wife and baby slept; soon another baby arrived
and the four occupied the bed. The kindness
which had been promised was noticeably lacking, except in letters home.

Annie at this time had not gained sufficient
schooling to be able to write a letter. She could
not have mailed it even had that letter been
written. She was a prisoner, a slave—a condition not uncommon in a day when orphans were
farmed out indiscriminately to almost anyone
who would provide them a home. But Annie
was not an orphan; she had not been "farmed
out," and her captors, to a certain degree at least,
felt the necessity of caution. They therefore,

each week, wrote a letter to Mrs. Brumbaugh, dilating upon the joyous existence of her child, and these letters were read to the girl herself, with acrid remarks when she remonstrated that she was not happy, that she was not willing to stay longer and that she wanted to go home. Then finally came a letter from Mrs. Brumbaugh, begging that her daughter be sent to her at once.

Misfortune once more had come to the family. The mother was ill, desperately so. The father had been injured; roads were poor in those days; it was far easier to use the right of way of a railroad to a "shortcut" near home, and while doing this, Brumbaugh had been caught in the center of the bridge by the approach of a fast train. Running in an attempt to reach solid ground before the train could strike him, he had stumbled and fallen to the deep gulley beneath, injuring a knee severely. Thus, with both heads of the household incapacitated, Annie was needed and needed badly. But Annie did not go.

A rather short letter was sent in answer to the plea, stating that the child was happy, that she had advanced greatly in school and that she felt that it would be an injustice to herself to return before her term was finished. One trifling thing was wrong with this. The child was not attending school—instead, as she washed the dishes, like a criminal with a smuggled manuscript, she studied a copy book which she had brought from the infirmary in a determined effort to teach herself to write, that she might someday manage to send a letter that would end her misery. But until then, she was as much of a prisoner as though the place were one of stone and steel; her every action was watched, even an absence of a moment from sight and sound brought the stentorian command that preceded search:

"Annie-e-e-e-e! You come back here!"

This condition continued for more than two years, during which time the child was kept in utter ignorance of the happenings in her own family. Her stepfather died without the child being given the knowledge, the home in which the Brumbaughs had lived was lost through a technicality of law, the family was to a certain degree disintegrated, neighbors taking the youngest of the children to raise while Annie's mother eked out an existence by working as a neighborhood nurse.

The slavery grew worse. Finally one night, nodding from fatigue—the child had been hard at work since early morning—Annie Oakley fell asleep over a basket of mending. It was the

34·

spark which ignited a smouldering blaze of animosity which had been growing for months in the breast of the wife of her captor. Like a flash, she was upon the child, to wrench her to her feet and with slappings and pinchings attempt to force her back to her work. Annie was in her stocking feet, and when she sobbed, after having been placed in the dark kitchen as a further punishment, the woman once more approached her, shook her angrily, then, opening the door, pushed her out into the frigidity of a mid-winter night. The ground was covered with a two foot fall of snow.

It was only one of innumerable cruelties. Time after time the child had begged to be allowed to return to her mother. The plea was refused, finally to be met with the statement:

"If you ask that again, I'll cut your liver and heart out and hang them on a fence stake for the crows to pick."

Nor was it wholly an idle threat; Annie Oakley's captors did almost as much. Such gentle little ideas as setting the clock ahead an hour so that the child would be at her labors at 3 o'clock in the morning instead of four, or of letting her go hungry during an attack of illness until the danger of starvation forced her to crawl down from her attic bedroom, were usual affairs with these kind, gentle souls who desired the cheery brightness of a little girl in their home. Her daily portion was slappings and pinchings, a command usually bore one or the other. And when a real beating came, it was with a whip, cutting so deep into the child's back that the welts remained red-green for months; the result of one beating remained with the child for the major portion of a year!

Therefore, with these precedents, a slight cruelty like throwing a partly clothed girl into the deep snow of a zero night apparently affected the woman but slightly. It was not until the man of the house returned that the child, nearly perished from exposure and cold, was allowed to return to shelter. Then, she was treated with something approaching kindness—the punishment had gone too far and the child was in delirium. At last, when she had recovered from the effects of her experience, her mind was made up, to escape, no matter by what means.

The opportunity, however, did not come until late spring. One day Annie Oakley found herself alone; the man and woman of the house having been called away. Practically penniless, she started forth, found her way to a railroad station and there, upon the arrival of the train, boarded it. Having no money with which to buy a ticket, she told her story to the first man who would listen, who paid her fare as far as the train went and left money with another passenger to carry her to her destination.

But there disappointment greeted her. The house which she had known as home no longer sheltered the Brumbaugh family; for the first time she heard of her stepfather's death, of the misfortunes which again had overtaken her family, and of its removal to a small place some twenty miles distant. Former neighbors of her family cared for her that night; the next morning at daybreak, stalwart, determined, the girl started out, walking her way homeward.

That day she got as far as the abode of the family of Joseph Shaw, some five miles from her own home, and the guardians of her tiny sister Emily. Shaw was a widower, and had a contract for the carrying of the mail some forty miles along the string of tiny settlements to the railroad. More than this, he had saved his money, and possessed a good farm, a small number of really domestic cows, a goodly number of horses and other attributes which, in this wealthless community caused him to pass as "well-to-do." Several times, since the loss of her second husband, Shaw had asked Mrs. Brumbaugh to become his wife, but she had refused his suit. Perhaps his wealth may have had something to do with it—fate seemed to have cast the mother of Annie Oakley for a constant role of poverty. It was at Joseph Shaw's home that Annie stopped, there to learn that her mother had gained the position of district nurse, a task of much work and little remuneration, and that she now was confined upon a contagious case and would not be home for some weeks. It was natural that Annie should be asked to remain at the Shaw home; this she did, and began to attend school immediately.

Two weeks passed in happiness. Then her former captor appeared one day at the school, having trailed the child who had dared to leave his home of gentility and kindliness. Against the remonstrances of the teacher, of Annie and of her playmates, he led her forth, under the insistence that she was "bound" to him until she was eighteen. But the return journey led past the home of Crawford Edington, the superintendent of the infirmary, and conditions forced the man to halt there for luncheon. The child hurried to her one friend, "Auntie" Edington— Mr. Edington being away. There was a hasty summoning of farmhands, followed by a scene such as one might expect in the third act of one of the old time thrillers, and Annie Oakley was safe at last from three years of slavery.

But she was homeless in a degree, penniless. Those years of slavery, however, had increased the agility of fingers already skilled to the needle. There was need for a sewing woman in the Edington home, that the supply of dresses might be kept up for the inmates of the infirmary, and the child applied for the position. More, she was able to keep to the requirements; soon she was saving money.

Incidentally, it was not long until the child had assumed the role of a juvenile reformer. Affairs were run somewhat loosely at the infirmary; although there were plenty of chickens and cows and a good supply of butter, eggs and milk, these things in some strange way failed to reach the aged and infirm to whom they should have gone. Edington was away a great part of his time. His wife was overwhelmed with a myriad duties, and when she failed to watch, thievery of supplies was rampant. Annie Oakley asked, in addition to her other duties, for the job of custodian of the dairy products.

Whereupon she put locks upon springhouse and storehouse doors, instituted a sort of requisition system, and proceeded to save products for the aged, the young and the infirm that had long been missing from the tables. Then, as she sewed on the dresses for the infirmary children, she begged for a few yards of turkey red yarn.

"For what?" asked the wife of the superintendent.

"To sew on the cuffs and collars," was the reply.

It was a new thought, speedily granted. From a child had come the suggestion that, for the first time in the history of one county institution at least, gave a touch of brightness to clothing that heretofore had been as bare of trimming as the clothing of a convict.

It was not until New Year's that she saw her mother; distances that today are nothing meant the travel of days in a time when there was nothing but the horse and the old "spring wagon," rutty roads and discomforts. Shortly after that, Annie went home to live—and work. Her mother had married for the third time—to more poverty.

Joseph Shaw had lost everything except his mail route. A scheming doctor, adept in persuading others to sign papers, and more adept in suggesting that the savings of a lifetime be given into his keeping, had seen to it that the frugality of Joseph Shaw reverted to his advantage and not that of the man who had done the

saving. Shaw was now practically penniless,
save for the earnings of his mail contract, which
were small indeed. Although it may sound
facetious, it seems inevitable that the world must
have so many good souls who are never so afflicted themselves that they cannot bear more;
such appeared to be the case with Annie Oakley's mother. However, that marriage was a
fortunate one, not in its apparent qualities; for
outside the fact that the new Mrs. Joseph Shaw
seemed perfectly happy with her third husband,
there entailed the usual fight for an existence, the
building of a new home upon a new farm, and
the inevitable struggle of a family to once more
get on its feet—an action, with the Mozee brood,
it seemed, which always led to being toppled
over by misfortune again. Therefore it was not
this which was fortuitous. It was the fact that
Annie Oakley's rifle must be brought into play
to save a household, and the reputation begun
which made her the most famous woman of her
type.

Chapter Three

THERE are certain elements in the story of the life of Annie Oakley which make one think less derisively of those old "meller drammers," where the oily villain strokes his black mustache and the mortgage hangs forever, like the sword of Damocles, over the "old home place." Yet, in a certain degree, these melodramas were true to the period and the places which they represented. Sixty years ago was a gullible period in American history. Then the sewing machine agent thrived, traveling the rural districts in his spring wagon, and eager to sell the best sewing machine on the market for a mere pittance, if the buyer would only pay a slight installment, signing a contract for the remainder. Thousands of notes were signed in this fashion, for the cost of the machine upon the face of the document, but in reality for a sum many times that amount upon a duplicate note carefully concealed beneath the true one, with the edge of the paper so cut that the gullible buyer signed the second sheet instead of the first. Sharks existed in every business, and in every avenue of

42.

From an early woodcut.

life; the usual banker was a usurer, demanding often as much as twenty-five per cent interest and getting it—even more; sometimes the rates ran as high as ten per cent a month. To one who has not delved into the absolutely haphazard aspect of America as it existed just before and after the Civil War, conditions seem utterly unbelievable. There was practically no regulation, as it exists today, no prying of officials into the business of others that this business might be kept within the law; there was corruption of the type which met its high water mark in later years with the statement of "the public be damned." Among the rank and file of humanity, there was practically no knowledge of law, such as exists today even with the comparatively uneducated. Anything which savored of the legal was looked upon, in rural districts at least, with a wholesome awe; in Annie Oakley's notes, for instance, there is an excellent instance of this in reference to the years of agony which she endured at the hands of a man and woman who were no more than slavers.

"Mr. Shaw left home with the intention of squaring accounts with The Wolf, but a suit for kidnapping would have to be brought up, together with expenses and no end of going back and forth for trial, so he was talked out of it."

So much for the adjudication of a felony. Such things happened often—fear of the law, of lawyers, of courts forced more than one person to accept injustice. Today, when a mortgage falls due, for instance, there is little excitement about it. One knows that the law provides that the foreclosure, unless there be a specific clause to different effect, means the sale of that property for the amount due, not the garnering of an entire security when perhaps only a tenth of it remains to be paid. But laws were different in other days, the protection was to the lender and scant attention was paid the borrower. A mortgage was a mortgage, and it was collected upon, either with money or the property, when it came due. There was no fuss about it, few renewals and little else expected than the fate of utter loss if the cash were not available to wipe it out. It was the ogre of rural America, was the Mortgage, and of course there was one upon the new home of Annie Oakley.

Since he had lost everything and since the mother had nothing save her flock of children, three of whom were now approaching marriageable age—sixty years or so ago, sweet sixteen often meant a marriage license—there seemed nothing to do but to build a home from the ground up. Shaw evidently had pretentious

44.

ideas, even though he was short of money. The
new home was the biggest that the family ever
had known; neighbors came from far and wide
to assist with the setting of the logs, real sawed
lumber was used on the interior, a carpenter-
contractor was hired, his price being a mortgage
upon the entire place, which children, grown-
ups, friends and even acquaintances had helped
to build; so fevered had been the exertions that
the children put down the well, of a depth of
twenty or more feet, by lantern light. When the
place was done, there was comfort in plenty,
and money—not at all.

Except of course, that which Annie Oakley
had earned and saved as a sewing maid for the
orphans and indigents at the home of the Ed-
ingtons. However, much of this money was
gone now; almost her first act when she had left
the infirmary to go to the aid of her mother and
new stepfather in the building of a home, had
been to stop at a store in Greenville, where, on a
few occasions, some of the overflow game which
the child had trapped as a child had found its
way to be traded for more necessary staples.

There was a better market now for game, the
storekeeper had told her; hotels in Cincinnati
and other cities were reaching out farther and
farther for the necessities of their menu; wild

game, a few generations ago, formed one of the chief lures of an eating place. Now it would be possible to ship any game killed, such as quail, rabbits, squirrels or pheasants to the store by the stage which ran near the new home of Annie Oakley, where it would be purchased, and then re-sold to hotels. A new avenue and a lucrative one loomed before Annie Oakley. To be paid for doing the thing she loved!

The result was that practically every cent of her store of money departed during that visit. When she left for home, she carried with her a conglomeration of traps, powder, shot, copper-toed knee boots, heavy clothing and a new gun. From that time on, her every spare moment was spent in the field.

The girl did more than learn to shoot with the skill of an expert. She became physically hardened, lithe, able to take to the field early in the morning, a heavy shotgun upon her shoulder, not to return until nightfall, when, loaded with game, she would arrange for its packing in hampers, and then, this done, aid with the housework with never an evidence of fatigue.

She was the tomboy of the family. When she brought the cows home in the evening, it was by a method entirely her own, that of grasping the last one by the tail, and then with shouting and shrilling, force it to speed, while, feet dangling, she volplaned in its wake. The fractious, half wild creatures, resentful of milking, yielded to her when they would submit to no one else; more than one miniature bull fight was staged by the girl as, dodging the rush of horns or the stamp of hoofs, she would so wear out an animal that it was glad of the opportunity to at last loll into a corner and submit to the approach of the milk bucket. Work was the lot of Annie Oakley from early morning until late at night; physical energy was hers to be exerted, and there were plenty of opportunities.

The country in which Annie Oakley lived was what now would be called a paradise of game. Thickly wooded, yet plentifully supplied with hills and dales and "draws," with brush piles resultant from newly cleared lands, hickory groves where the squirrels chattered incessantly, corn and grainfields, it formed a fit roving place for a dozen forms of small game. These paid the mortgage on the farm; long before the allotted time was up, Annie Oakley had placed in the hands of her mother and stepfather the necessary money to wipe out the incumbrance, and the family entered upon a period of prosperity which it never before had known—all because of a muzzle loading shotgun in the hands of a girl not yet thirteen years old.

Hunting now had become almost wholly the girl's life. She loved the bark of the gun, she loved even more the clearness of open country sunshine, the nodding white of the elder-berries against the staggered rails of the hickory fences, the deep, cool recesses of the walnut groves, the murky somnolence of the slow-moving creeks, where one might place a trap and obtain skins that would bring a return in money, once they had gone to market. She loved the tang of frost in the air, the harvest moon shining over the cornfields, the deep red of the sumac bush, re-painted by the first touch of cold weather, the cheery color of the red-haw tree, loaded with its autumn fruit; and more than all this, strangely enough, she loved the animals which she para-doxically killed.

Perhaps it was that love which, coupled with incessant practise, made Annie Oakley the best of all women shots. She hunted for market, it is true, and there was nothing unsportsmanlike about it in those days when game was abundant and when the popular idea was that it would exist forever. But in that hunting, a certain softness of heart made itself ever apparent, far better was it to give her quarry a long chance

48.

and lose a bird than to take a "pot shot" and possess just another bit of dead game. The result was that Annie Oakley soon found herself an adept at difficult wing shots—so, being an investigative little soul, she tried still more intricate ones. It was not long after this that the word began to spread of the shooting ability of Joe Shaw's little stepgirl, who, on each stage day sent great hampers of quail to market, and who, by her prowess with the shotgun and rifle, was giving to the family a prosperity that was unusual for the community. Spurred by her efforts, others began to hunt for market, but the game which Annie Oakley dispensed always commanded a better price. It was cleaner killed and better handled—her prowess permeated beyond the little store which acted as a commission merchant for the produce of the field and woodland. It went even as far as Cincinnati. And by the time three years had passed, there was good cause for her standing as a local celebrity.

Annie Oakley had not been satisfied with just shooting. Roaming the fields with her gun, she tried various tricks, such as turning around a time or two when a bird rose, and then shooting as she spun into position. Or taking a run, a skip and a jump with the bird on the wing, just to see, in child fashion, whether she could accomplish this, fire and bring the quarry to earth before it had sped out of range. This and a half hundred other things that a child would think of, she practised, "just for the fun of it" with never a dream that it would go farther. This was during a time when, following the building of the Kansas Pacific Railroad across the Great American Desert, a man, having made his reputation as a buffalo shot, and as a scout for Phil Sheridan, Custer and other famous generals of the plains, was beginning to reap a golden harvest by appearing in plays of the wild and woolly west, such as "Scouts of the Plains" and other endeavors where the crack of the rifle was far more emphatic than the lines which the actors uttered. It was Buffalo Bill, already becoming widely known through his plays, through the publicity given his efforts for the feeding of the workers on the Kansas Pacific railroad and through the stories of Ned Buntline, which, although rarely true, were certainly blessed with an accumulation of imagination.

Shooting was more than a mere fad in those days. It was regarded as a high accomplishment and as a distinct aid to life. The Civil War had done its part to make persons familiar with fire-arms. Then too, there was the constant hullaba-loo concerning the Indians, which, however friendly they might be at the time, could at any moment—in the opinion of haphazard newspaper correspondents—arise upon a final rebellion, and strive to wipe the white man from the face of the earth. The West was a predominant topic of conversation—sooner or later, practically everybody expected to go there and reap a fortune for the mere taking of a trip. Booms it seems, must be with us always. As Florida and California have occupied public attention, so the West occupied the waking and dreaming moments of the eastern populace during a period which, to say the least, was unsettled.

The war had come and gone, leaving dissatisfaction in plenty in its wake, as is the case with all wars. For years there had been the frenzy of conflict; now with the coming of peace, a people could not, all in a moment, swerve back to the old, accustomed viewpoint. Farmers made homes and cleared the brush, only that they, in the vernacular of the day, might shut the door of their cabin, whistle to the dog, call the kids and be on their way to a new clearing and a new adventure. The covered wagon was an actuality; free land was calling in the West, the mountains were beckoning; the common topic of conversation between families would be when they started out to make their fortunes, in answer to the command of Greeley: "Go West, young man!"

Naturally, to go West, meant to undergo hardships and dangers, both real and imaginary, the greatest of these being the wild animals which were supposed to lurk behind each butte and mountain, that they might lick their chops over some human victim, and the Indian, whooping his cry of war as he descended upon the innocent paleface who was doing nothing more than ruining his hunting grounds. This all had its part in the stimulation of interest in shooting, and few indeed were those who were unable to draw a bead along the lengthy barrel of a squirrel rifle and fail to hit a mark at a dis-. tance which might be called phenomenal in these days. Therefore, when Annie Oakley stood forth from the common herd of shooters, it was because she had accomplished unusual things.

The natural amusement of a small, backwoods town was the shooting match. Perhaps the turkey shoot, or the rooster shoot, or the prize shoot —it was as popular as golf today. There came the time when Annie began to enter these contests, usually managing to take home the prize, and her position as a crack shot became gradually more confirmed. Hotel keepers, who were wont to buy the produce of her hunting expeditions, heard of her. One especially took a keen interest in the Darke County girl who, with rifle or shotgun, on foot or from the back of a horse, could easily outshoot men who had given years to practise. This had a sequel.

Into Cincinnati, when Annie had reached fifteen, came the far-famed team of Butler and Company for an engagement at the local opera house, performing deeds of daring and dexterity, with firearms, the billboards doubtless said, seldom exhibited before the eyes of an audience. There was little difference between fifty years ago and today as regarded the necessity of publicity for a performer; Frank E. Butler often augmented the attendance at his performance by challenging the local celebrity to a shooting match on the morning of his show and then, having thoroughly beaten him, inviting the audience to come, one and all, to the opera house that evening where one could see shooting that was shooting. His partner did likewise, but this particular match concerns Butler alone.

Naturally, with his arrival in Cincinnati, the usual subject of a local match, with a side bet— there were always side bets on a shooting match —was broached, to bring about a quick rejoinder from the owner of the hotel at which Butler was staying.

"I've got a shot I'd like to put up against you," the hotel keeper said. "For a hundred dollars a side."

It suited Butler. However, he naturally was curious regarding the contestant, and asked the name.

"Oh, it's someone you never heard of," was the answer. "The name wouldn't mean anything."

The arrangement was made for the contest, then, somewhat dubiously, the hotel keeper went forth in search of Annie Oakley, with the promise of a chaperoned visit to a big city—the first one she ever had seen—and all her expenses for the trip, to say nothing of half of the stake if she should happen to win the meet.

It was something to ask—of anyone but Annie Oakley. The prospect of a big city did not seem to frighten her whatever. Nor the fact that she was about to meet in contest a man who was a good enough shot to make his living by performing on the stage. In fact, Annie Oakley thought it over heavily, and then went into conference with her younger brother concerning financial matters.

Three older sisters had married now and departed for other homes, leaving Annie at fifteen the oldest of the children and a sort of unofficial head of the household, inasmuch as by her earnings she had made it possible to enjoy an unwonted prosperity. She was the mainstay, the balance wheel, tomboy though she was; upon Annie devolved many of the heavier problems of the household. It was therefore something of a risk to take savings which might be badly needed and wager them upon her prowess in a match with a professional sharpshooter.

But the spirit of adventure was strong upon the two children. They pooled their every possession. Annie Oakley sought the hotel keeper with the announcement that she would not only shoot the match, but that she thought well enough of her chances to bet fifty dollars upon the outcome.

It was a wildly excitable journey, that trip to Cincinnati. Big buildings, real trains—not the chugging, side-line affairs which she had known in her district—crowded streets which seemed a bedlam to a country girl, and at last the shooting grounds in a park near Fairmount, where a rather surprised performer looked with a little more than ordinary interest toward a lithe, small bodied girl, with a wealth of chestnut hair, who had busied herself with an inspection of the shooting boundaries.

"Who's that pretty little country girl?" asked Frank Butler.

"The one you're to shoot against," came the reply, followed by introductions. It was a propitious meeting.

Trap shooting, with clay pigeons, had not yet come into vogue. This match was to be with live targets, one barrel to be used, and gun below the elbow—in other words, held down so that it must be raised to the shoulder as the bird left the trap. About the time that the final preparations were made, the referees stepped forward, and the toss of the coin made to determine the first shot, an affliction smote Annie Oakley. Strange spots floated before her eyes. Her tongue grew suddenly dry, cleaving to the roof of her mouth and refusing to leave. Her knees shook, why she did not know. Stage fright affects one that way. Blankly she looked toward the spectators, toward her mother and brother and sisters, gathered there, to see their Annie shoot. Through a haze, a figure approached his trap, called "pull" in an even tone and then dropped back, gazing professionally through the wreath of smoke which had burst from the muzzle of his gun.

"Dead!" had called the referee and the match was on. About that time, Annie Oakley forgot stage fright, relatives, and all else, save her muzzle loading shotgun.

56.

"Pull!" she cried and the trap sprang.

"Dead!" came the monotonous tone of the referee.

They talked about that match for a year in Cincinnati, how it ran bird for bird, shot for shot, until at last, an instant of poor aim on the part of Frank Butler caused him to drop one point in the rear. How, steady now, eyes keen, every action perfect, a fifteen year old girl called her signal and dropped her bird, no matter how swiftly it flew, how sharply it quartered, or how instantaneously it rose. To the twenty-fifth bird they went, and Frank Butler raised his gun for his last shot.

"Dead!" called the referee and the score was tied. Then Annie Oakley gave her command. Her old muzzle loading shotgun boomed.

"Dead!" Again came the call, in announcement that a girl from Darke County had won her first professional match. But nothing was said about other things. How was the referee to know that she had also won a husband, and fame that would travel world wide?

Chapter Four

FRANK BUTLER was an actor with the soul of a
poet, and with an eye to the unusual. This had
been different from the ordinary match; in the
first place, it seemed worth losing a hundred dollars to discover a person of Annie Oakley's unusual attainments: a fifteen year old girl who
could come out of the wilderness, poorly dressed,
apparently at sea with her surroundings, and
then, all in an instant, summon the concentration to shoot a successful match against one who
had every advantage on his side. Frank Butler
did not halt his acquaintance with the paying of
the match money. Instead, he insisted upon
meeting the girl's mother, her sisters and brother
and then his carriage ready, invited them to ride
downtown to luncheon, only, of course, it was
called dinner then.

It must have been a rather unusual meal.
None of the family was versed in what might
be called "city manners." It was the first time
the guests ever had seen the interior of a big
hotel. At far worse odds than when she gave
the command for the pulling of her first trap,

58.

Waiting for a target . . . and the photographer.

ANNIE OAKLEY

Annie Oakley underwent the agony of striving to pick a meal out of the maze of a printed bill of fare, noting vaguely that upon this very menu were noted the game birds which she had killed in Darke County and shipped to market.

An amazing luncheon in fact. To be waited upon by obsequious servants. To see glittering glassware and shining silver lavished about in what seemed the display of a veritable treasure vault. To note the people who came and went —the rest of that day was hazy to Annie Oakley. The night was even more so; for the cheerful loser of the match had bequeathed the entire family passes to his performance and Annie Oakley attended her first show.

The girl occupied a rather strange position at that performance; she had defeated the man who was on the stage, yet she saw things there which she never had dreamed of being able to do, tricks of stagecraft, manners of presentation; Annie Oakley's idea up to this time had been that "shootin' was shootin'" and that frills did not count. However, she learned differently this night—if, in the maze of watching the most wonderful performance in the world, she could pause to differentiate. But even in spite of her excitement, there were things which she could not help noting; how a comparatively easy shot at a simple target, for instance, could be made difficult by the introduction of an element of danger. In Frank Butler's act was a French poodle named George, whose part in the performance was to walk to a pedestal, hold himself rigid while an apple was balanced on his head and then, when the shot was fired which broke the apple, catch a bit of the fruit between his teeth, walk to the footlights while the applause roared and then, having satisfied the audience that he was a canine target of a modern William Tell, retire to the back of the stage and champ upon his fruit until the performance was finished. Viewed in its cold light, the trick was a simple one. The marksman already had hit far smaller objects; a target the size of an apple was nothing for him to strike with a rifle bullet. But it was the element of danger, the thought in the mind of the audience that if Butler missed in his aim, a dog would be killed. Since the audience never had seen a dog killed in just that way, it was thrilling. That night, Annie Oakley, always a veritable blotter when it came to the quick absorption of a theory, gained her first lesson in showmanship. She also gained something else. She left the theater with the firm idea she had become terribly interested in a dog.

After the performance, Frank Butler had sent

60.

for his guests and brought them backstage. There, shy, excited, not admitting to herself that this man whom she had defeated in a professional match, only that she might marvel at him when he had appeared in the halo of footlights and a stage presentation, had impressed her whatever, Annie Oakley, in true country girl style, had lavished her entire attention upon George, the French poodle. He was the most wonderful dog in the world according to her conscious calculations, and when at last the trip was made back to Darke County, she carried a promise from George, detailed of course, through Frank Butler, that the dog would send word every now and then regarding his happiness and how the act was getting along. The promise was kept. "George" wrote to Annie Oakley and Annie Oakley wrote to "George." A third-hand wooing entirely. Frank Butler was a young man at the time, much Annie Oakley's senior, when years were concerned, yet only in his twenties withal. The country girl with her dark eyes and wealth of chestnut hair, her determined manner of tackling the task in hand and carrying it through to a conclusion, her evident self confidence in the face of conditions which might have made another backwoods girl quail, her evidences of unswerving courage—

and Annie Oakley possessed that quality to a remarkable degree—all these things had made a distinct impression. And Frank Butler had impressed Annie Oakley. Or was it George?

As far as anyone knew, it was the latter. That a dog should be an actor was a marvelous thing to her; straightway, in child fashion, she strove to make thespians out of the various canines which lolled about the farm, but without much success. They didn't seem to possess the theatrical temperament; perhaps the distraction of fleas had something to do with it, or the fact that they were just "dawg." This failing, she tried other things which had made their mark upon her brain; the trick shooting, the hitting of objects in spite of handicaps; that day in Cincinnati had been the outstanding event of her life and, as she roamed the fields in search of game, she visualized herself in costume, before footlights and an audience—childlike reproductions which, however, were to have their sequel. It was not long before Annie Oakley realized that she could do everything that had been performed upon the stage. But her theater was the vastness of meadow, the rustling defile of a weed filled draw, the semi-darkness of the walnut grove, her spectators paradoxically her targets.

Autumn came and Christmas. With the holiday season arrived a present from "George," in the form of a box of candy. Then as time and other presents arrived, the subterfuge was dropped. The next August, Frank Butler went to Greenville, where he was met by Annie Oakley. They were married, and after their honeymoon, which consisted of travel from town to town as the engagements of Butler & Co., dictated, Annie Oakley turned to the achievement of a life ambition. Now, married, with her living provided for her instead of waiting for the crack of her rifle or the black-powdered explosion of a shotgun, she could do that for which she had longed always. She could go to school!

There is a pathetic undertone to the notes of Annie Oakley, written sketchily in after years, often with the true story of her existence hidden in a rambling account in which she referred to herself sometimes in the first person, sometimes in the third and sometimes so cryptically that it is next to impossible to ascertain about whom the notations are made. That undertone refers to an education; the longing for it was with the girl always; even when a kidnapped slave, beaten until she could neither sit nor lie upon her back, so deep were the welts given her as a Christmas Eve benefaction, there had been the copy book and the speller, a determined child striving to

63.

teach herself the rudiments of things she believed necessary. Here and there during those same notes are glorious references to two weeks at this school, or two weeks at that, sketchy attendances, which, however, stood forth like great events, when, old and white haired, Annie Oakley looked back upon her childhood and wrote of it. With her marriage came the first opportunity to study which she ever had known, and she sought it avidly. Among other things was music.

It already has been mentioned that Frank Butler was a poet of a sort, and beyond that an unusual type of man. Before his meeting with Annie Oakley, he had met only two persons who had been able to defeat him at shooting, both of these nationally known crackshots. He was a performer, with an actor's natural feeling of necessity in the furtherance of his own personal popularity; ego is to a certain extent an absolute necessity for any actor. It is a jealous business, dependent greatly upon how often one's name appears before the public. Therefore, there is no sacrifice like that of the actor, ready and willing to subdue himself that another may take the honors.

But Frank Butler had fallen in love, that day of the match shoot. A strange beginning, to

64.

love the girl who has defeated one, stranger still that with this chance meeting there should have ripened an affection that should end in marriage. Not that it has not happened oftimes and many—but when the continuance of that marriage runs along the lines of Frank and Annie Butler, it represents one of those miracles which happen seldom enough to form an outstanding case. Only death separated the pair, and that after more than forty years in which gradually, but surely, Frank Butler had dropped more and more into the background, content and happy if but the world give to the woman he worshipped the homage he felt she deserved. Nor was this affection a reflection of fame; Frank Butler had always loved Annie Oakley with the sense of protecting worship unusual even among those generally credited with a happy married existence.

In preparing for this recital, the biographer had cause to investigate a stack of letters, aged and yellow. Some were of no consequence, others gave little sidelights into the story of a woman, who carved an unusual niche for herself in the world. And among other things was a wrinkled, broken bit of blue-ruled tablet paper, upon which the ink had faded, but on which the words

were still legible. It was a poem by Frank Butler, bearing the date of Quincy, Illinois, May
9, 1881, and the heading:

LITTLE RAIN DROPS.

There's a charming little girl
She is many miles from here.
She's a loving little fairy
You'd fall in love to see her.
Her presence would remind you
Of an angel in the skies,
And you bet I love this little girl
With the raindrops in her eyes.

Some fine day I'll settle down
And stop this roving life;
With a cottage in the country
I will claim my little wife.
Then we'll be happy and contented,
No quarrels shall arise
And I'll never leave my little girl
With the raindrops in her eyes.

At the bottom of the aged piece of paper was
an almost boyish notation:

"Written and composed for my little girl by her
loving husband, Frank E. Butler."

While on the other side, in faintly pencilled
words was the afterthought, evidently accompanying a gift:

66.

ANNIE OAKLEY

"Now you can wear this to church Sunday, as I am going to send it now. Aren't you my little girl?"

This was long after the first connubial arbor had been given plentiful time to cool, for Frank Butler and Annie Oakley had been married some five years. Five years, incidentally, in which many things had happened in the career of the girl who was to become the world's foremost feminine shot.

The schooling, upon which Annie Oakley had embarked immediately after her marriage had been doomed for an abrupt end. Butler's partner had become ill, on the eve of a featured engagement at an important theater. Naturally, there was a conference, ending with the suggestion of Butler that his young wife take the stage with him, thus relieving the act of being a solitary one, her sole duty that of being the object holder and general assistant. But Annie Oakley demurred.

"I don't see why I should do that, Frank," she said, according to the notes made by her of the incident. "I can shoot as well as you. I think I should be able to go on and trade shot for shot with you. You take one shot while I hold the object for you, and then I take the next one, you acting as object holder for me."

It was a matter of import, to a young pair, about to embark upon a "team act." Frank Butler's presentation had been fairly successful; true, the young pair drew no tremendous salaries; "variety" in those days was not a highly paid profession. But at least the act had provided a living; to attempt a change in it might mean disaster. The decision was finally made, however, to make a try of it, and, taking insurance against mishaps, adopt a subterfuge in case the first performance should fail.

The aid of the manager of the house was therefore enlisted, that he might make an announcement to the effect that since Mr. Butler's partner had become ill, a young woman from private life had volunteered to attempt to fill the role left vacant by the incapacitated performer. Annie Oakley appeared in her street clothing; no such thing in those days of taking the risk of purchasing a costume which might only be worn once —if the act were a failure!

It was the first time that she ever had appeared on the stage. There had been no rehearsal; there was no sense to one. Annie knew her husband's act; as far as she could see, there was nothing to do but shoot, and all the rehearsal in the world could not help with that. The uncertainty of appearing before an audience, shooting by artificial light, the knowledge that upon her work and hers alone depended success or failure —these things may have entered the girl's calculations, but she said nothing of them.

That was an attribute of Annie Oakley, that she took nothing into consideration save her determination to do the thing upon which she had set her mind. A strange combination of human nature, this little woman of Darke County beginnings. As mild as an April shower, apparently as unsophisticated as though she had come but yesterday from the backwoods which produced her beginnings, kindly to a point that went far beyond the usual definitions of thoughtfulness, her nature contained also a quality that savored of the strength of steel. Perhaps it came from the exigiencies of her youth, the trials, the sufferings; perhaps it was ingrained from a mother who had been forced to smile in the face of misfortune for the greater part of her life, but it was there; a sublime form of self-confidence, wholly without ego, which caused Annie Oakley, once she had considered a feat or a task, to believe wholly and utterly that she could perform it—and then go ahead and do that which she believed! It was with this attitude that she looked upon a future career as a stage shot, and she went to her first performance with the assurance of one who had been doing it always.

She missed her first shot—the knocking of a small cork from the bottom of a glass, held in the hand of her husband. Quite calmly she studied her surroundings, noticed a difference in the light from that to which she had been accustomed, made allowances for it, raised her rifle and struck true and the act was a success. The next day the girl dug into her savings for the requisites of two costumes and the act became professionally Butler and Oakley.

It remained thus for some time as the pair, riding the day coaches that they might save every spare penny for the buying of costumes or some bit of scenery or stage dress, living at the theatrical hotels, where, in those days, one could subsist well upon ten dollars a week, and practising economy in every possible way, made the rounds of the theaters of the East upon what might now be called harem-scarum tours, Frank Butler writing ahead and describing his act, and their route dependent largely from one week to the next upon what bookings had arrived by the last mail.

Gradually, however, conditions took on a more settled aspect. The bookings became more regular, and as the act became better known, the figure of Annie Oakley stood out more and more prominently. Frank Butler found himself in the position of one who received applause, only that greater applause might go to his child wife; steadily, surely, she took the position of the star of the performance, while her husband gave more of his time to coaching, and managerial duties. Now it was Annie Oakley who shot the apple from the head of George, the French poodle. It was Annie Oakley's name which took the place of honor in the advertisements, Annie Oakley who was watched for and commented upon by the audience.

And while she was slowly building her reputation there was coming into being in the West the background that someday would serve to carry her to even wider fields of endeavor. Buffalo Bill had served his time as the hero of thunderin' thrillers depicting everything from the adventures of the "Scouts of the Plains" to "Life in the Badlands" and the lifting of "The First Scalp for Custer." He had seen his name grow from that of a scout for the Indian fighting troops along the Republican and Saline Rivers in Kansas, to that of one who was looked upon in the United States as the typification of the West. Now, he was launching his first Wild West Show, and hoping for the best. His showman career was truly in its real beginning, as was the public life of Annie Oakley.

Oakley and Butler were known as a team of rifle experts, little more. They had advanced to the position which now would be called that of headliners; the tricks which Frank Butler once had done being cheerfully given over to his young wife, while he stood on the sidelines and beamed with a pride as fatherly as it was connubial. This during the theatrical season—when that was over, a child once more, Annie Oakley hurried to her books and school, feverish for that which had been denied her, an education. Then in the first years of the 80's came a happening which advanced her prodigiously, a bit of publicity as well-earned as it was fortuitous, but one nevertheless which gave her a standing that otherwise might not have come for years.

Sitting Bull, the Sioux warrior, and the accredited destroyer of Custer and his army at the Little Big Horn, was the outstanding savage figure of the day. Following the battle in which the wily medicine man had outwitted the forces of the United States Army and engineered the massacre which followed, Sitting Bull and various of his followers had escaped into Canada, where they had remained until various overtures

of peace had assured them that it would be safe
and wise to return to the United States. Treaties
had been talked of, there had been the usual
palavering of white agents who had assured the
old chieftain that practises of the past would be
abandoned and that a new day was dawning for
the Indian.

Baiting Poor Lo had been an exceedingly
popular sport for years; that and a general harvest of graft with the redface as the recipient of
the small end of proceedings. Every beef
weighed out to the half starved recipient of government bounty had been accompanied by two
men who also stood on the scales, thus reaping
a small harvest, not for the government, but for
contractors and agents who professed to love the
poor Indian, and perhaps did, inasmuch as that
Indian was the source of easily earned, even
though illy gained, wealth. Sugar was served in
what was known as half and half, the remaining
portion being sand. Rotten hams, rottener bacon,
all these things went forth to the Indian, to say
nothing of counting steers twice and other favorite little tricks with which the government itself
had little to do, but for which it was held
responsible in the eyes of the Indian. These
happenings, together with the invasion of the
Black Hills by the rush of gold miners in viola-

tion of existing Indian treaties, had brought about the rebellion which had carried its sequel with the Battle of the Little Big Horn and the annihilation of Custer. The usual result of an Indian war had been reversed, and the "massacre" had caused Sitting Bull to be looked upon as a combination of an Indian super-man and a fiery demon.

But whatever the opinion, there was no doubt of his importance. Sitting Bull typified everything that was fierce and savage, and all that was cunning. A thousand legends had sprung up about him, one whom he could recommend as being a great warrior, a great racer, or rider or shot must be all that and more, for he was the Indian of all Indians. Therefore the fortuitous circumstance.

Sitting Bull with his companion warriors, Rain-in-the-face, limping as a result of a wound received in the Battle of the Little Big Horn, Red Cloud, and Curley the Crow Scout, accredited with being the true sole survivor of the Custer Massacre, arrived in St. Paul, Minn., on their way to Washington to see the Great White Father and arrange with him for new treaties. Naturally their presence had been the signal for unwonted interest; St. Paul was as much engrossed with Sitting Bull and his chieftains as those chieftains were engrossed with the big city of St. Paul and the methods of living practised by the whites. The result was that they were taken everywhere and shown everything in which they expressed the slightest interest. One of the things which Sitting Bull had desired to see was a show, and at that show was—Annie Oakley.

A powerful old fellow, steeped in the ability of regarding things with a certain air of the judicial, Sitting Bull endured most of the performance with occasional grunts of *"Waste,"* indicating his approval or a running undercurrent of comment in Sioux with his companions which gave little indication as to enjoyment or disapproval. Then at last the act of Annie Oakley and Frank Butler began and Sitting Bull sat up with a new interest.

He could understand guns and shooting and marksmanship. He grunted at the first few efforts, and became more engrossed. Slowly his excitement intensified. Finally, as the house applauded one of Annie Oakley's more difficult feats, that of shooting the end from a cigarette held between the lips of her husband, the old medicine man arose from his seat, his heavy arms waving in wild gesticulation.

75·

"Watanya cicilia!" he shouted in Sioux. *"Watanya cicilia!"*

It meant "Little Sure Shot," a name which Sitting Bull often had applied to his own daughter, who had met death shortly after the battle of the Little Big Horn. But as Annie Oakley later described it, all she could think of was the name of a saint.

Time and again as the act progressed, Sitting Bull repeated the name, and then, the show over, proceeded stolidly to his hotel, where with a glance about his room and an examination of the gas lights, calmly lit his long-stemmed pipe, pulled in a mouth-full of smoke, puffed out each flame, and then, the room slowly filling with death-dealing gas, proceeded to roll himself in his blankets and prepare for sleep, resenting thoroughly the interference of the bellboys and the manager who hurried to rescue him. But he was not done with "Little Sure Shot."

He told the story of her prowess over and over to his braves. Following this, he held a council and decided that anyone who could shoot with such precision should be a member of the Sioux Tribe. But first he decided that he should have her picture and that she should have his.

Sitting Bull had not been averse upon his journey to making a few dollars for a minimum of work. No Indian ever is. Invade a Sioux reservation today and ask a stalwart brave to pose for his picture and he'll do so willingly— for a quarter. The same has been true always. Sitting Bull had discovered speedily that he was a personage, and with true Indian innocence, proceeded to cash in upon the idea. He had learned, with much scrawlings and jabbings of a pencil to print his name upon a card, and this, in answer to the desire of some paleface for an autograph, was cheerfully given in return for a dollar. Another accomplishment was the drawing of a very grotesque buffalo, which together with the printed name of Sitting Bull drew a little more from the paleface pocket than a mere signature. In this wise, since his arrival in St. Paul, Sitting Bull had garnered a pouch containing eighty dollars.

Following the council, the old chieftain dispatched a warrior with the pouch and a much larger drawing than usual of the buffalo, together with his signature, to Annie Oakley. The warrior interpreter also carried a message, to the effect that Sitting Bull wanted her for his daughter, in the place of the one he had lost— she too had been Little Sure Shot. The gift he was sending was in payment for one from her— would she send him her picture, and would she consent to become his daughter by adoption and a member of the Sioux tribe?

Annie Oakley sent back the money, her picture and her consent. The ceremony took place in the hotel, a weird, solemn gathering of befeathered Sioux, who conducted the ritual and pronounced an incantation over the young, somewhat amazed girl. Then a stick was broken over her head, the pipe passed from one red warrior to another. Sitting Bull gave to the girl a golden nugget, supposed to have come from a lost mine. Then the dance began, to the skip and the beat of the tom tom, in celebration of the addition of *"Watanya Cicilia"* to the Sioux Tribe, a daughter for Sitting Bull to take the place of one who was gone.

After that, theater managers were more eager than ever to book the act of Oakley and Butler. It was something quite important to be able to say that next week there would appear on the bill "Little Sure Shot," the adopted daughter of the medicine man who had engineered the now famous massacre of General George Armstrong Custer.

Chapter Five

THE new spurt of interest on the part of the public found a ready adherent in Frank E. Butler. Always in the background, prideful, eager, he sacrificed gladly, if by so doing he might advance the person whom he worshipped with a sort of love that seems all the stronger when contrasted with its beginnings, with the wandering, roving life which this pair led, the comparatively hasty marriage and unusual courtship. Viewed from the standards set by precedent and the general rule in such alliances, the marriage of Annie Oakley and Frank Butler should have failed. His interest in her had been aroused by the fact that she had been an unknown, coming from the backwoods in answer to a challenge which he constantly issued to "meet all comers," that she had shown the necessary concentration, the determination and the courage to defeat him at his own game and on a day, when, according to his own statements, he never was shooting better. Annie Oakley's interest in Frank Butler had been caused by the fact that he had been practically the first man of the world with whom she had come in contact, a man surrounded by the halo cast by footlights, the glamour of the stage, the mystery of having traveled far and seen strange things. To every marriage of this type which survives, there are a thousand which fail—but the alliance of Annie Oakley and of Frank Butler was the exception which proves the rule. For in all the world of exhibition, and especially of the tented world, where marriages are more "for keeps" than in the general run of life, the union of Frank Butler and Annie Oakley forms a criterion of happiness, due entirely, of course, to the fact that they were two natures who welded, who understood, who truly loved each other and who were happy— well, because they were happy. The unusual aspect of the match, however, was Frank Butler's attitude.

It would have been quite the usual thing if, having married this girl from the backwoods, he had "allowed" her to become a part of his act, subordinating herself to him. It was indeed unusual that, a performer in his own right, the stellar member of an act which already had won its right to appear as a feature in various theaters, he should voluntarily subordinate himself to her. Not that Frank Butler merely became "Mr. Annie Oakley." He did nothing of the sort. But he did, more and more, of his own volition, drop into the background that her star might shine the brighter, contenting himself with the knowledge that he could shoot true when he chose, and taking a greater pride in the applause that came for the "little girl with the raindrops in her eyes" than if it were for himself.

There is more to performing before the public than the mere performance. There is the managerial end, the taking advantage of every quirk and turn of circumstance, the handling of contracts, the making of bargains and the incessant haggling for the proper payment for services rendered. Frank Butler was an experienced man of the stage; he knew far more of these things than Annie Oakley, and as time went on, he veered more to that end of the business, working quietly and efficaciously, taking her praise for himself and leaving the plaudits of the multitude for her.

A broader field now presented itself, and a year or so after the Sitting Bull episode, there came the opportunity to join a circus at a greater salary than either ever had known in the theatrical business. More, it promised steady employment and a freedom from the somewhat haphazard life of leaping hither and yon, the disadvantages of stages of different size, lighting arrangements that were precarious at best and many other inconveniences.

Not that the circus was a millenium. Far from it. This was in 1884, when tent shows were far from the efficient pieces of amusement machinery that they are today, and when the moral aspect of circus life was indeed a different affair from what it now presents. This is not in reference to the performers, but to the circus as a whole, for the history of the bad reputation which traveling tent shows once endured, concerns two entirely separate ingredients.

One was that of the performers, the persons who really gave the show, a clean-living, clean thinking, simple folk who had little or nothing in common with any other element. Their lot was not an easy one; for in addition to giving the performance, helping with the raising and the lowering of the tents and the setting up of paraphernalia whenever bad weather, late arrival or any other misfortune beset the show, they were the ones who must also suffer the contumely for that which they were in no wise responsible. They were the ones whom the populace saw— the people thought nothing of the trailers, of the "kid show" grafters, of the workingmen, recruited often from low stratas owing to the niggardly wages which were paid in those days for laborers of the circus—sometimes as low as two dollars a week. The public only knew that a circus was a circus and given by performers; ergo these performers must be the ones who committed the depredations which usually happened about the time that the circus came to town.

Today, there is no need for extra policing, except for the handling of crowds, when a tented organization comes to a city or village. There is no need for plain clothes detectives, watching the personnel of the show, to garner criminals which may be riding with the organization in an effort to escape from some other city. Neither is there need for the ardent housewife to forego her washing day if it should happen to fall upon the same day as that of the exhibition, unless it should interfere with her desire to see the show. Nor is there the necessity for the nailing of windows, the extra locking of doors and the maintenance of a guard upon the house while the rest of the family hies forth to see the animals. The circus of today, with one or two outstanding exceptions—outstanding because they are so rare—is a thoroughly clean organization, as wholesome from a standpoint of law observance in its every department as it once was wholesome only in the personnel of those who formed its performers, and who, through long generations of necessity, had lived clean lives for the very reason that if they had not, soft muscles and excess softened brains might mean their death during the action of their risky acts. This change has come about within the scope of little more than a generation, owing to the activities of five brothers well known to the world as the Ringlings, who, with the start of a few dogs and ponies, or even less, fought their way to the topmost rungs of the amusement world, and gained much of their impetus by their resolve to build a circus at which anyone could be safe. But, back in the early eighties, there were few such organizations.

There were "trailers," who rode the show train, turning in a certain portion of their illicit earnings to the owner of the show. There were petty thieves and clothes-line robbers. There were "cappers" and "grafters" and "shell artists" and all the rest of the merry crew, which, holding forth in the sideshow, mulcted the gullible visitors by every possible means, from three card monte, to straight out and out confidence games, which often were consummated with the aid of the local banker, himself not above taking a percentage of the gains for his reward. The bribery of public officials to look the other way while games of chance went on, was not at all unusual. In fact, one "fixer," as the gentleman was called, who arranged matters with the local police, and even with city councils, gained a reputation for never having told a lie.

"Gentlemen," he would say when he faced the council with a request to allow certain "games and amusements" to proceed under the sheltering tents of an approaching circus, "there seems to be some objection to my little plan on the grounds that we are coming here to run games of chance. I wish to deny that statement. A game of chance is something where there is an opportunity on either side to win or to lose. There is nothing of this kind with the circus.

"What we purvey to the general public is in reality an educational department. There are a certain number of yokels in the world who believe that it is possible to get something for nothing. Without our aid and assistance, they might go through life forever without becoming the wiser, thus causing distress and suffering of the most widespread character. Now, our task is to teach these reubens that there is no such thing extant. They come to us, believing the statement that they can get something for nothing. When they go away, they do so with the knowledge taught by us, that such a miracle is not possible. That is our educational depart-

85.

ment. It is not a game of chance. If you can find any device, or game, or contest under the sheltering spread of our broad and benevolent canvas that gives the sucker even a ghost of a chance, I shall be glad to buy each and every one of you a new hat. Gentlemen, I thank you."

To such a life went Annie Oakley, speaking in the broad sense of the term, for Annie Oakley went with a circus. Whether the show with which she first cast her fortunes possessed the usual attributes in the way of clothes-line robbers, petty thieves, grafters, "shills," short-changers, "booze camp" keepers and the rest of the pirate crew, it is not for this writer to say, inasmuch as there is no personal knowledge on the subject. But that type of show was the common one in those days, with the exception of course of Barnum, Ringling and a few others. Fights among the workingmen and townspeople were not unusual, and the status of a circus performer certainly did not touch the highest rung of society's ladder.

And there are certain indications in Annie Oakley's notes which would indicate that this particular circus was not of an extreme moral character. The performers were illy treated. Such devices as the holding out of two weeks' salary, presumably to be paid at the end of the

season, but usually dissipated through the inflic-
tion of petty fines for real or imaginary offenses
against circus rules, cheating upon the provisions
for the performers, the charging of wholly
visionary advances for costumes, wardrobe and
anything else of which the management might
think—these things were all present, and for a
time Annie Oakley and her husband endured
them that they might later, even though in a
small way, become reformers.

The beginning of it all was a sentimental one.
A young bride, unused to the professional world,
had come to the show with her husband, signing
a "generally useful" contract, as it is known.
"Generally useful" is a department of circusdom
devised for performers who are neither stars nor
gifted with any performing ability that will
make them stand out from the herd, as well as
for persons who can perform a number of acts
which aid in the general ensemble. The bride
had agreed to be "generally useful," believing
that about the extent of her duties would be to sit
atop a horse in parade or in the general tourna-
ment or entry. But, when she found herself
equipped with an ancient side saddle with a
broken horn, a horse which seemed none too
tractable, and the necessity for executing the difficult manouevers of the "rose garland entree,"

a sort of equine quadrille requiring at least some knowledge of equestrianism, she adopted the usual bride expedient and sat herself upon a bale of hay and wept.

Here the resolute, perky little "Miss Sure Shot" found her and inquired the cause of the tears. After the explanation had been given and Annie Oakley had expressed herself regarding the management of the circus, she announced that since she had nothing to do until the time for her act came, that she would take the bride's place in the entree.

It was fun for Annie Oakley, born to a horse, and little caring from childhood whether she had a saddle or not. But since a saddle was a part of the equipment and since this was a circus which was supposed to treat its employees with something resembling humaneness, Annie Oakley asked to have that saddle repaired. The request was refused. Then, one day, the little crack-shot noticed that the girth was in shreds. So she too sat herself upon a bale of hay.

Entree time came. Annie Oakley still kept her place on the hay pedestal, while beside her sat Frank Butler, ready for all comers. The bugle blew for the beginning of the entree, but the entree didn't begin; whereupon the manage-

ment of the circus asked the reason. It came
with the simple statement:

"Annie Oakley's out there, sitting on a bale of
hay. She won't get on her horse and she won't
go in entree. She says she won't budge until that
saddle's fixed."

The manager hurried for the "back door"
where was assembled a circus's entree, all dependent upon a resolute being who, backed by
her husband, still held her place on the hay bale
and invited trouble.

"That saddle's all right," came the bawling
announcement.

"Is it?" asked Annie Oakley and leaped from
her position. A quick yank and she had seized
the girth. The rotten threads parted; the saddle
dropped to the ground. "Not until that saddle's
fixed do I go in entree!"

When Annie didn't go in entree, it meant
there wasn't any. The "rose garland" could not
be executed with less than twelve riders. That
afternoon the show proceeded without its opening feature, while one of the first circus strikes
in history went merrily on, led by a little woman
who had learned in childhood how to be
adamant. The next day the strike was over; the
saddle had been repaired, and a slightly different
attitude toward performers was evidenced by a

management which previously had viewed this department with but scant attention.

It wasn't the only time that Annie Oakley proved herself a stormy petrel in this first year of her circus experience. Often only afternoon shows were given, there being no adequate method for lighting at night, and the show was not equipped with the train sleeping conveniences which exist today. There was no "cookhouse," on this particular show, where the performers gathered for their meals; instead, they were "contracted" at various hotels, the cheaper the better in the opinion of the management. Until one day, the performers were thrown into a place which was little more than a brothel. Again Annie Oakley took to the warpath; again conditions changed.

It was during this tour that Annie Oakley and her husband visited New Orleans, there to play an engagement in the same city in which the primary opus of Nate Salsbury and Buffalo Bill was exhibiting to business which was far from enthusiastic. Naturally there was an interchange of visiting between the shows, in which the Butlers saw an amusement enterprise which strove at least to be different from the usual run, and, with the exception of the inevitable roughness among its workmen, depart from the time

Colonel William F. Cody,—"Buffalo Bill."

dishonored idea that a circus was merely a background for gambling devices and general chicanery.

Buffalo Bill had ended his first season as a showman a much sadder, wiser and poorer man. When the first year was over and the losses had been counted, a friendly disagreement had arisen between Cody and Dr. Carver, his partner, resulting in a breaking of their business arrangements. Whatever may be said of Buffalo Bill as a showman, he was never a show manager. He was the picturesque figure, the actor, the romantic appearing typification of the great West out of which he had come and which he loved to the day of his death; in this role he was pre-eminent. But in the niche of a show-maker and show-executive, he was sadly lacking. There was too much of the dreamer in his make-up, too much of the hale-fellow-well-met, too little of the shrewd, calculating far sightedness necessary to the man who would start a tremendous organization upon its tour and make the plans, months ahead, that would bring it safely home again.

Colonel Cody had done much of the planning of the first season. The plans had failed. A mere gathering of buffalo, of cowboys and vaqueros and Indians, of stagecoach holdups

and this, that and the other thing; the show had
little purpose, little endeavor and little accomplishment. Then too, the embarkation had been
an absolutely new idea in showmanship. The
type of performance with its many shooting
events, which would have ruined an overhead
canvas, precluded its being given in the usual
circus tents. The idea of a side-walled arena
had not been perfected, with the result that the
show had been forced to exhibit in fairgrounds
and places of the like, during the afternoon only,
owing to the lack of an adequate lighting system,
and often far from the town proper, making the
distance prohibitive to a great many persons who
otherwise might have been spectators. The
season had been wholly negative, leaving Colonel Cody with little more than an idea.

And with one other thing, the necessity for a
real showman, who could assume the managerial
tasks while he looked after the presentation of
the performance, and this man had come in the
person of an actor-playwright named Nathan
Salsbury.

Salsbury had proved himself a genius of sorts.
He could write a play if a play was necessary,
and held the record of having done so in eight
hours. He could manage a theater, or a theatrical company, taking it through the vicissitudes

which then attended every thespian adventure without ever an appearance of worriment. And he could, when he chose, book himself as a comedian and command what then was an outlandish price for his services. Cody had met him while appearing in Western melodramas, and following the practical collapse of his first venture in the outdoor exhibition field, had made overtures to Salsbury to become his partner.

The arrangement had been made and the show started for New Orleans, for a winter's exhibition at the Exposition Grounds, while Salsbury, knowing that money might be needed to carry on the venture, continued in the field of the theater, appearing with a company called "Salsbury's Troubadours," then in Denver. Under his advice and management, efforts had been made to lift the show into a position out of the ordinary. A program had been arranged, with something of theatrical sequence, persons who were well known in dispatches from the West, had been hired, new equipment bought and the show had been refurnished to a point which had eaten deeply into the resources of both men. It had therefore been disappointing when Salsbury, about to answer his cue in the performance of the Troubadours, received a telegram stating, in characteristic Cody language:

"Outfit at the bottom of river. What do you advise?"

That was exactly the status. The show had been placed aboard a Mississippi River steamer for transportation to New Orleans and had been proceeding merrily upon its way when an obstruction had risen in the shape of another steamer. There had been a collision, damaging the showboat so severely that she had sunk in less than an hour. Now, wagons, camp equipment, arms, ammunition, buffalo, an elk, and, in fact, everything, save the old Deadwood stagecoach, the horses, which had been swum to safety by the cowboys, a bandwagon and the performers, lay at the bottom of the Mississippi. Salsbury's action in regard to that telegram may give one an inkling as to some of the reasons for the early success of the Buffalo Bill Wild West. The orchestra was sounding his cue for a song as he read the message. Hurriedly he reached for the speaking tube.

"Play that over again and a little louder," he ordered of the orchestra leader, "I want to think a minute."

And as the music was repeated, Nate Salsbury wrote the answer to the grief stricken message of Cody:

94.

ANNIE OAKLEY

"Go to New Orleans, reorganize and open on your date."

It was while the show was recuperating from its pre-opening misfortune that Annie Oakley and her husband visited it. Not too alluring a prospect, this stricken affair; true, most of the losses had been made up, a new herd of buffalo procured and equipment added to take the place of that which had been swallowed by the Mississippi, but there was an air about the entire assemblage that was disappointing. The Exhibition, of which the show formed a part, had not lived up to the dreams of its promoters. Attendance had been poor, consequently the wild west show had suffered; two hundred Indians, cowboys, vaqueros and a certain scout of the plains were anything but cheerful. But there was one thing about the performance which Annie Oakley and her husband noticed—that was the kindliness with which every performer seemed to be treated, and the personal interest which Buffalo Bill took in his organization from trick rider to the merest pounder of a stake. Somewhat different from a place where one was forced to lead a strike in order to insure the protection of a saddle that would at least stay on a horse, and the Butlers began to wonder if they would not like to become a part of a Wild West.

Correspondence began shortly after that, but of a disappointing character. The end of the season in New Orleans had found Buffalo Bill and his partner Nate Salsbury with sixty thousand dollars less than when they had started, to say nothing of the impending expenses for the opening of a new season. The Buffalo Bill show, therefore, could not afford to pay the salary which Butler had asked for his wife; the time had come when Frank Butler was willing to withdraw entirely from a standpoint of performance if his "little girl with the raindrops in her eyes" could only have the homage due her.

But Annie Oakley and her husband were determined to go with the Buffalo Bill Wild West. This in spite of the fact that if she were given the engagement, she would be the only white woman with the entire assemblage. At last the correspondence reached a point where Annie agreed to come on the show for three days, exhibiting for that time. If, at the end of the period, she had not proved her worth to the show, the exhibitions were to be free. If, however, the opposite were true, she was to receive the salary asked.

They met the show at Louisville, Ky.; the

grounds were deserted, save for a few attendants and a man whom Frank Butler and his wife believed to be merely an onlooker, who stood at the end of the grandstand in the fairgrounds where the exhibition was to be given.

"Everybody's out on parade, I guess," said Annie Oakley. Her husband moved with an idea toward their trunks which had just been delivered to the grounds.

"It'd be a good time to run through the act and see how you get along," he said. "You'd get some practise for the afternoon."

Annie Oakley liked the idea. Together, before the empty grandstand they arranged their traps, pulled forth a table to act as a standard for the various guns, brought forth the faithful French poodle, George, for his William Tell act and proceeded in the belief that they were holding nothing more than a rehearsal. Meanwhile the quiet appearing man at the end of the grandstand merely stood and watched.

One by one the figures of the act were gone through, Frank Butler acting as the object holder and trap puller. The glass balls traveled into the air, at first singly, then in pairs and finally in triples and doubles, all to be crashed by quick shots from Annie Oakley's rifle before they could touch the ground. Then the tricks

which she had known on the stage were practised; the shooting of a mark with the sight being taken in the bright blade of a bowie knife,
the throwing of objects into the air to be knocked
down after Annie Oakley had turned completely
about, firing even before she came to a standstill.
Then the quiet appearing man walked forth
from the end of the grandstand.

"Your name is Annie Oakley, I take it," he
said.

"Yes."

"Have you a photograph—something with
your gun?"

The woman hesitated and looked at her husband.

"Why—I haven't anything recent."

"Then would you mind if I called a cab and
sent you down to have some tintypes taken?"
asked the newcomer. "My name is Salsbury.
I'm Buffalo Bill's partner. I'd rather have tintypes, if you don't mind. They reproduce
better."

"But—."

"I'd like to get a letter off today," insisted
Nate Salsbury. "I think about seven thousand
dollars worth of printing would be sufficient,
don't you?"

On the way downtown, Annie Oakley came

to a true realization of what it all meant. The "printing" would be for billboards—her picture, looming beside that of Buffalo Bill and his Congress of Rough Riders of the World. Seven thousand dollars was a sizable amount in 1885. The question of salary was over now. Annie Oakley had entered a rehearsal—and emerged a star.

Chapter Six

THE introduction of Annie Oakley to the life she was about to assume as the only white woman in the entire wild west company of Buffalo Bill was a typical one—such as only Buffalo Bill or Nate Salsbury could present. Showmen both in their every waking moment, they could not overlook an event like this. Consequently, when the parade returned to the grounds, Indians with feathers flying, cowboys with their chaps and sombreros and spinning lariats, Mexicans and herdsmen and buffalo ropers, squaws and pappooses and *travois*, there was a quick conference between the showowners, followed by a bugle call for immediate attention. Hastily the entire assemblage formed in line. Then Nate Salsbury took his place on one side of the woman who was to become the greatest shot in the world, Buffalo Bill advanced to the other. The Colonel raised his tremendous "four gallon" hat—it was known then as a sombrero.

"Boys," he announced, "This little Missy here is Miss Annie Oakley. She's come to be the only white woman with our show. And I want you boys to welcome and protect her."

It was thus that Annie Oakley gained the name of "Little Missy," used affectionately to her death by her intimates. Buffalo Bill called her that at the beginning; he used no other name for her in the seventeen years of their association with the "Wild West." And in her notes, Annie Oakley describes that introduction as one of the high spots of her existence.

"My husband and I were introduced as one of them—the first white woman to stand and travel with what society then might have thought impossible. Every head bowed. I felt something like a wild gooseberry sticking in my throat as the friendly, rough hands covered mine, one at a time, as they passed. Then the chiefs, followed by their tribes, passed with a *'How! Waste!'* meaning 'all is good.' A crowned queen was never treated by her courtiers with more reverence than I by those whole-souled Western boys."

Annie Oakley, in all her years with the Wild West, never had cause to recant that statement. A cool headed, resourceful, deliberately courageous person in the ring or at the traps of an exhibition shoot, she was after all, once work was over, just a child-woman, viewing the great world with the eyes of one who had been denied much in her childhood and now that more fortunate days had come, strove with almost pitiful eagerness to absorb, all in a few years, the wonders which she had all her life been denied.

A child-woman in more ways than one; after all, she had foregone a childhood, such as others know. Long hours over the sewing basket, longer hours over knitting, the wandering of field and dale, heavy, muzzle loading rifle upon her shoulder that she might provide a living for those who depended upon her skill with firearms for the very necessities of life, the arduous hours in which she had prepared her game for market; that and her years of work, both as a virtual slave and at the infirmary—these things hardly could be classed as the innocent, buoyant amusements of childhood. But now, married, a star in a tremendous organization which, although it had seen the darker side of conditions in its beginning, speedily was to forge forward as one of the really big amusement enterprises of the world, the Little Missy could revert to things she had lacked and longed for. She could play!

In the Buffalo Bill company was a frecklenosed boy in a big sombrero, who, today, lives beside the grave of Buffalo Bill, on Lookout Mountain, near Denver, and who talks much of

102.

Annie Oakley. His name, like that of Little Missy, was a familiar one a generation ago, for he was classed as the champion male rifle shot of the world. He is Johnny Baker.

A boy then, following a god whom he never deserted, either in the physical or spiritual sense, Johnny Baker had looked upon Buffalo Bill as the Alpha and Omega of life. His home had been near the tremendous, rambling structure of the Cody Home in North Platte, known as "Scout's Rest," and with the beginning of the plans for the first Buffalo Bill show, Johnny Baker, with the goggle eyes of a youngster looking upon marvels unbelievable, had followed the every rehearsal, held, incidentally, in quite casual fashion, down by the railroad station. Then, at last, as the show prepared for the road, he had gone to the scout and asked:

"Please, Buffalo Bill, can I go with your show?"

Colonel Cody had looked down, pompously. He had ruffled his goatee and shaken his long, heavy hair. Then in his booming voice, had asked:

"You? Go with my show? Why, blast my skin, Johnny, what could you do with a show?"

The freckle faced boy had hesitated, but only for a moment.

"Well," he had said, with an inspiration, "I could black your boots!"

It all had ended with the addition of the freckled Johnny to the personnel of the Buffalo Bill Wild West Exhibition, but not as a bootblacker. The boy always had been a favorite of Colonel Cody, now, with one of those typical Cody impulses, he became a foster parent to the boy and started him on a career as a rifleman.

"Might as well learn while you're young!" he boomed. "I did."

That had been the start of Baker's career, with a god in the form of Buffalo Bill to be patterned after. Now, in a tremendous sombrero which all but unbalanced him, his hair growing long, just like Buffalo Bill's, he practised daily with the rifle and the lariat, the boy of the big show. Annie Oakley joined him as a playmate.

The children of the Indians which accompanied the show formed the rest of a childhood coterie. That season, after the long parades, and following the hours of practise which both Baker and Annie Oakley put in at their rifles and shotguns, the exhibition grounds resounded to the sounds of more juvenile antics, such as the wild shouting accompanying "Run Sheep Run," or the squeals and screams of a game of "tag" with sloe eyed Sioux maidens and giggling Indian braves-to-be taking a rather blank part in it all, while drawling cowpunchers watched or gave advice, and stoical bucks puffed their pipes on the sidelines. A strange combination this woman, now in her twenties, practising at attempts to break world's records with a shotgun, playing at childhood games—and planning to attend school again when the show season ended that winter!

Soon the friendship between Johnny Baker and Annie Oakley in kidhood games became also a friendship of the arena—a rivalry which lasted, in fact, for seventeen years. Who, of the old generation, does not remember the thrill of kidhood, when, legs dangling over the hard edges of the "blues," male pride forcing one to take the championship of Johnny Baker, the stocky little man and the slight girl came into the ring, to shoot, as Buffalo Bill expressed it, twice daily, rain or shine, for the championship of the Buffalo Bill Wild West.

Boys—of air-rifle shooting age—were the greatest exponents of these two. Forms bent, hands clasped, eyes centered, they sat in the general admission seats, sans popcorn, sans peanuts, sans program, for their one and only twenty-five cent piece had gone for the purchase of the general admission ticket, watching this "titanic

battle for the supremacy of male over female"
for the "championship" of the Wild West. Day
after day was that championship decided, and
day after day the argument was reopened, with
the coming of each performance. Perhaps to
the elders who watched it merely for the skill
portrayed, it was only an exhibition. But to the
youngster on the "blues," and the writer must
confess that he was on more than one occasion
an ardent rooter, it was a life and death affair,
where chivalry demanded that youthful support
be given the almost frail little woman, while the
feeling of sex supremacy, coming down from
ages gone, tugged oh so hard, that Johnny Baker,
by some miracle, pull out from the lead which
the girl was taking over him. But, one after another the glass balls traveled into the air, to be
cracked by the steady stream of fire from Annie
Oakley's rifle, and Johnny, try as he might, lost
the match.

An argument inevitably followed this contest
as the last rush of the Wild West was over and
the seats emptied—a battle of words which
lasted long after the hoof beaten oval of bare
earth had returned to grass and Buffalo Bill's
Wild West Show had traveled on, to places and
scenes remote. That was as to whether Johnny
Baker hadn't just let her win after all. Whether,

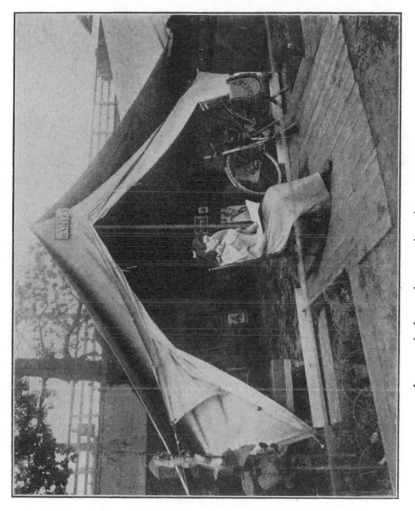

At ease before the tent in winter quarters.

they hadn't "fixed it up" beforehand, so that she would be the "champeen" of the Buffalo Bill Wild West.

Years and times bring vast changes. This writer, once one of the howling mob which filled the "blues," was thrown by circumstances into the companionship and close friendship both of Buffalo Bill and Johnny Baker. The Buffalo Bill show, as such, was a thing of the past. Annie Oakley, white haired, had retired from the arena.

We were at the edge of the Bad Lands in South Dakota, upon the spot, where in the ending years of the last century, Big Foot and his band of half-starved, graft ridden Sioux braves, had met the military in the last Indian Rebellion, the Ghost Dance War which had resulted in the Battle of Wounded Knee. It was Sunday. Buffalo Bill sat in the opening of his tent, surrounded by army generals of Indian fighting days, old scouts, Sioux braves, each vying with the other at the telling of some tale of days long gone. Johnny and I were at one side, Johnny with a rifle, and I with a handful of half-dollars, bequeathed by various visitors to the camp—we were on a motion picture expedition—to be thrown into the air, plunked on the wing by a shot from Baker's rifle, and then held as souvenirs. And while in this temporary job of "object thrower" a sudden reversion came to other days, and a subject which for years had remained unsolved.

"Johnny," I asked. "Tell me something. When you used to shoot against Annie Oakley, and she always won, was it because you weren't trying, or because she was a better shot than you?"

Johnny sent another half-dollar spinning, then looked seriously toward me over the barrel of his rifle.

"There never was a day when I didn't try to beat her," he said. "But it just couldn't be done. You know, the ordinary person has nerves. They'll bob up on him in spite of everything; he'll notice some little thing that distracts his attention, or get fussed by the way a ball travels through the air. Or a bit of light will get on his sights—or seem to get there—and throw him all off. I wasn't any different from the average person, but Annie was. The minute she picked up a rifle or a shotgun, it seemed that she just made a machine out of herself—every action went like clockwork. And how was a fellow ever to beat anybody like that? To tell the truth," Johnny drawled, "it would have made a better show if I could have beaten her every few performances. But it couldn't be done."

But at the time Annie Oakley joined the Buffalo Bill Show, the idea of such contests had not yet come into being. Johnny Baker was still a boy, and only learning to shoot. Annie Oakley had her set act and went through that—the one which she and Frank Butler had performed on the stage, meanwhile practising for other things.

The cowboys and their tricks entranced her; almost with the adoption of her by the entire company as a sort of little sister—the name Little Missy came naturally, once Buffalo Bill had applied the nickname—there was also a voluntary kidnapping. The cowpunchers—green hands straight from the range, most of them, and widely different from the showman style of "waddie" which one now sees with the various rodeos and round up exhibitions, regarded the girl with a mixture of awe and affection. And with the moment that she evinced a desire to learn the tricks of their profession, there was a surplus of bow-legged, wide hatted teachers.

One by one they gave her lessons with the lariat. They taught her the western style of riding. They taught her the reasons for bits of costume which seem theatrical to one who does not know the West, but which came about through sheer necessity instead of a love of the spectacular—the high heeled boots for instance, with their heavy curve under the instep, built to support the foot in long hours of riding, and to hold the heel from sliding through the stirrup when a western horse decides to stop and turn, all in its own length. The big hat, built for shade from the blistering rays of western sun, for a roof in time of rain, wide enough to throw the dripping dampness beyond the collar and to the protection of oil-skin slicker, instead of down one's neck, to say nothing of a drinking cup for man or beast in time of need; the bandanna, conceived to keep the dust out of one's collar, the stiff gauntlets to hold one's cuffs from catching in the twist of a thrown rope, thus bringing the danger of being yanked unceremoniously from the saddle; the chaps for protection from brush and thorn-weed, dryness in time of rain, warmth in cold weather and blizzard; the wide "stock saddle"—a rocking chair to most easterners, but exceedingly necessary when one works on a horse, instead of merely rides. All these things they taught her, together with the theories of the lariat and the spinning rope, how to keep that rope from kinking by keeping it turning with the left hand in synchronization with the movements of the right, and a hundred other tricks of cowboydom that are as necessary to the art of "ropin' a critter" as a knowledge of the alphabet is necessary to writing. Annie Oakley had found a new phase of life in which to become interested; her schooling in the early days of the Buffalo Bill Show, superintended by drawling cowpunchers and the gutteral applause of Sioux braves, played a tremendous part in her later success. When the Buffalo Bill show swerved into the tide which ran it to success, Annie Oakley was of the West western, as much of a typification of the Western girl to the audience as Buffalo Bill was a typification of the ideal Western man.

But these were the days before success, the days of embryo, of planning, of hopes and dreams and difficulties. The Buffalo Bill show at this time was by no means a finished product.

Usually, one show a day was given, and that in the afternoon. Then, the slow process of loading the train began, with the journey to the next town. Sometimes, these journeys were short, allowing the performers to go to a hotel for the night, but often, owing to the slowness of transportation, the exigiencies of loading and the necessity for sidetracking that regular, scheduled trains might pass, the daily trip was more often of nightly duration. And for this a makeshift sleeping arrangement was conceived. The backs of two seats were tilted up and fastened securely; then three cushions were put in place, one at the head and two lengthwise, long boards being carried under the seats to hold these cushions in place. Over this a mattress was placed and of course, bed clothing, each performer who desired a bed of this type, furnishing his own equipment.

As an example of the rather precarious form of sleeping accommodations which this arrangement afforded, the boy whose duty it was to make the beds, was late to work one rainy night. As he hurried about his work, he discovered that two of his precious boards were missing. The train stood by a high fence, and the boy strove to take a few standards from their fastenings, but failed. Then he climbed the fence and grunted with a discovery. He had found his boards.

The next morning, Annie Oakley arose after her sleep of the night, gazed rather drowsily at the protruding end of the board which had supported her couch, blinked, looked closer, and turned hurriedly for her husband. Together they raised the bed and gazed upon the support in its full perspective. Then they shouted for the boy.

112.

"Where did you get this board?" asked Annie Oakley.

"Why on the other side of a fence in the last town."

"Well, you wrap it up and send it back! What's more, you're going to hear from Buffalo Bill for this!"

He did. The reason being that the board had been a white one, with a rounded top, bearing in black lettering the words:

"Here rests in peace
the remains
of
Joshua Pepper."

However, hard as the life was, the performances often being given in the rain—it was the lot of any Buffalo Bill performer as long as the show lasted to appear in downpours, even in snow, owing to the fact that the ampitheater, during the whole life of the exhibition, was an open one—it was not because Buffalo Bill did not strive to make things as pleasant as was possible under the circumstances for his little "shooting star" and her husband. Two private tents were carried by the show, one of which was for Colonel Cody and Nate Salsbury; the other was for Mr. and Mrs. Frank E. Butler. In this tent were folding chairs, a steamer chair, a rug, a chintz curtain and light cots and blankets, a collapsible bath and other conveniences, which Annie Oakley could enjoy when she was not busy with her performance, her childhood games with the Indians and Johnny Baker, and her practise with the cowpunchers. That she proceeded well with this latter was evidenced by the fact that before the season had well progressed, Annie Oakley could rope and hold the wildest horse the show possessed.

From town to town the Wild West was progressing, on "one day stands," and these cost the act of Butler and Oakley one of its prized possessions. That was George, the amiable French poodle, which had acted as the intermediary of marriage of Frank Butler and Annie Oakley, and which had accompanied them upon their various adventures. Old now, somewhat feeble, life had been harder for George on the Wild West. Instead of being boxed for a journey once a week or perhaps at a more infrequent period, it was a daily matter. One day as Butler and his wife careened through a blinding rainstorm on the way to the train, the old dog faltered and fell. Hurriedly the pair called a cab and that night, sat beside a being that was more than a dog to them. Show people are sentimental—with George there were reasons. It had been this dog which a backwoods child had used as her shield in writing to a man she loved, this dog whom an actor had enlisted as an aide to marriage; George who had formed for years an integral part of their act, and who often had received as many press notices in the earlier days as they. The dog died that night. The next day, a wild west show held a funeral.

Upon many a showlot, scattered throughout America, there stands, hidden away from the prying investigation of the inevitable boys who scour the grounds after the show has departed, a home made little headboard, announcing a name that sounds foolish to the passerby, but which has meant much to the show which has come and gone. It is the grave of a pet—perhaps the goose which has followed a clown about the ring, a dog, now missing from one of the acts, buried there by showfolks who showed almost as much grief over the parting as they would have done for a human. Animals are peculiarly close to the heart of a performer; it is an ingrained affection which dates afar back, into the days of the mountebank, when with his trained bear, his performing baboon, the amusement vendor stood by the roadside, living by the pennies tossed him in recognition of the antics of his animal companion. More than one clown has this writer seen with the tears on his cheeks as he buries a companion, more than one mournful dressing room disconsolate while the band plays on in the big top and the acts flash from ring to aerial and back to hippodrome. So it was with George, and the Wild West became anything but hard-hearted with his death.

Two hundred men were they with that show and but one white woman. But that day, the assemblage, rough as it undoubtedly was from a standpoint of society standards of the age, might have been feminine in its entirety. Glum cowboys fashioned a box, then waited, tongue tied, while Annie Oakley and her husband placed within it the body of a poodle dog, resting upon pillows which once had decorated the stage during his act. Over in the tepees of the Sioux, a queer, wailing chant rose, the ghost song, voiced as Indian girls worked over the wreaths that would rest upon the grave of something that to the ordinary mind was only a dog. Then, at last, the procession, to a private lawn, where by appeal, a space had been granted beneath a spreading pear tree, that a beloved member of an act might not merely sleep in the expanse of an exposition grounds. Two cowboys carried the box there, others followed, and stood about,

116.

bowlegged and silent, their big hats weaving in rough hands. Those of the cynical might say it was foolish—but the cynical do not know the loneliness of the show business, they do not feel the aloofness, the knowledge that all of life is a wandering, restless thing where existence depends upon the mood of a populace, and friends are friends often only as long as the applause continues to ring. A dog is faithful. An audience is the most insincere, cruel, heartless thing that exists. A performer has his right to grieve for a true friend.

On went the show and the Butlers with it, working gradually East, and with a steady succession of plaudits for the work of the girl who now formed one of its stellar attractions. True, of course, there would have been no Buffalo Bill show without the presence of Colonel William Frederick Cody. There would have been no successful tours without the brains of Nate Salsbury, his shrewdness in arranging the route of towns to be visited, his ability to foresee in which places money would be plentiful thus making it possible for persons to attend an amusement enterprise, his showmanship which gradually was rounding the performance into more and more of the spectacle which it later became and his managerial capacity which gave to the assemblage a coherence which Cody could never have accomplished. But in addition to this, there was another ingredient which played a tremendous part in the growing success of the "Bill Show" as it was coming to be known. That was the presence of Annie Oakley.

The fact that she was the one white woman with the organization counted for much, especially when it was considered that she was slight, weighing barely 110 pounds, young, pretty and of the most feminine appearance. Then too, there was the prestige added by the approval of Sitting Bull, which, Major John M. Burke, the press agent and life long worshipper of both Cody and Annie Oakley, did not overlook. Besides all this was the marvelous character of her work, often performed in rain and storm, with the thunder crashing and the lightning literally playing about the steel barrels of her firearms. Little is needed as confirmation of her popularity, save a typical review, copied from an age-yellowed edition of a Chicago newspaper:

"There is a swift breaking of ranks and the kaleidoscopic marching and countermarching of the galloping horsemen back and forth till they vanish at last in the mimic mountains at the north of the grounds. Annie Oakley, a girl who has made her-

self famous with the rifle, has suddenly appeared.
No one knows where she came from, but there she
is, while the last "rough rider" is still in sight, and
there are her guns. A couple of young men have
arranged her traps, and she bows to the grandstand,
then turns to shoot. She makes a pleasant picture
down there in the great quadrangle. She wears a
short skirt, a tight-fitting costume, a cowboy hat and
the entire buckskin appearance of her garments adds
to the picture of the frontier lass.

"She is wonderfully accurate, breaking composition balls with an almost unerring accuracy. Two,
three, four balls are thrown into the air at one time,
and she breaks them, changing her double barrelled
gun in the midst of the feat. And she is determined.
She places her rifle on the ground and walks back
some twenty feet. The trap is sprung and she runs
forward, snatches up the gun and fires. She is trying to break both balls. But the time is too short
and she misses one. She tries it again and again.
It seems beyond the possible. But she does it at
last, and the whole, great audience repays her with
generous cheers. When she has done, she bows
widely to the audience and runs like a deer across
the hundred yards of space to the flies. Every movement in that dash across the square is a certificate
to the value of the school in which she has learned."

The amusement world has not changed much;
it still likes to see the impossible become the possible, and because of that, a trick of the trade
lives forever. Annie Oakley missed the same

number of times at each performance; strange wasn't it? And strange too, that the same trick still endures; the gymnast of the circus or the vaudeville show always receives a greater ovation on a difficult trick—when he fails the first time! Such is showmanship.

Annie Oakley knew that, and as a showwoman she became an indispensable part of the show, then really in process of true formation. Nor was the time long until she became of equal value in still another respect. For without her, the Buffalo Bill Wild West might have missed one of its most unusual features of the early days, and one which again served as a rung upward. That was the presence of Sitting Bull.

Chapter Seven

THE idea of capitalizing the Battle of the Little Big Horn, more familiarly known as the Custer Massacre, through the presence of Sitting Bull, had existed for some time with Cody and Salsbury, but the question of his coming had always been answered with a decided negative on the part of the old warrior. Sitting Bull had no desire to be a member of the Wild West Company; he felt that the white people looked upon him as an enemy, and, for that matter, *Te Tonka Ua Tocka,* which was his true Sioux name, had no especial reason for looking upon the paleface with any heightened degree of affection. Therefore, whenever the question had been broached by agent or emissary, Sitting Bull had refused and allowed that, as far as he was concerned, to end the matter.

However, Cody and Salsbury were insistent and at last, in the summer of 1885, sent another emissary to him with instructions to argue until the medicine man had changed his mind. This was not an easy task. For three days the conversation was entirely one-sided. The agent had been selected with care; it was Sitting Bull's interpreter who had served on the trip East when the warrior had met and adopted Annie Oakley as "Little Sure Shot" and given her as a memento of his affections, the moccasins worn by him during the Battle of the Little Big Horn. These moccasins had been made by the daughter who had died, and Indian fashion, Sitting Bull could think of no more fitting present.

As has been mentioned, the conversation for three days had been one-sided: The interpreter told of the great *Pahaska*—it was Colonel Cody's Sioux name, meaning "The Long Haired Man,"—and the esteem in which the Indians held Buffalo Bill as a great warrior and a good friend. He had dilated upon the wonderful experience of traveling about the country with a Wild West Company, the sights to be seen, the money to be gained. To all of which oratory, Sitting Bull gave a thorough answer. He said, "No."

The matter came to a point of despair. Then the interpreter noticed that whenever a brave of Sitting Bull's command desired something, he got it. The "open sesame" seemed to be to enter Sitting Bull's tent, converse about various topics and then, taking a position before the cabinet photograph of Annie Oakley, given to Sitting

*So pensive, yet so bold,—a profile study that was displayed
wherever the show went.*

Bull during the St. Paul meeting, dilate upon the wonders of "Little Sure Shot," and go into a general resume of the incident when Sitting Bull had adopted a daughter to take the place of one he had lost. By the time the process of amelioration was over, the interpreter noticed, Sitting Bull was in a beaming state of amiability. Then it was that the favor was asked, as quickly granted, and an Indian sent happily on his way. The interpreter decided to try the same methods.

He too stood before the photograph. He too sounded the praises of *Watanya Cicilia*. Having done this, he asked Sitting Bull how he would like to see his adopted daughter. The old chieftain changed countenance entirely. That was something very much desired.

"Then come with the Wild West show and you can see her every day," the interpreter said. "Little Sure Shot is with the show. She wants to see you too."

Shortly after that, there sounded throughout the camp of Sitting Bull, the high-pitched, yet gutteral call of the camp cryer, as he went about with important news:

"Enokone eupo! Enokone eupo!"

Freely translated, it means a little of everything, from the demand for attention on the part of every inhabitant of a Sioux camp, to the need for hurry, for gathering about, for making ready for travel or whatever else an Indian desires to interpret it along such lines. In this instance it presaged the giving of great news. Sitting Bull wanted his chieftains for matters of great moment. A council was to be held and at once. The ruse of the interpreter had been successful. Within an hour, with all the solemnity which only an Indian chieftain can know, the agreement had been made and sealed. Sitting Bull, with forty of his chieftains, would become a part of the Buffalo Bill Wild West. And all because of Annie Oakley.

A great day, that day of arrival, for Sitting Bull. There was his daughter, and there were the wonders of a Wild West exhibition; it was not long before the old Indian had become a seasoned trouper in every sense of the word.

A good hearted old fellow, this wily medicine man, to judge from the notes of Annie Oakley, a bit amazed by the progress of the white man, and to a certain extent, a Communist.

"The contents of his pockets," say those notes, "were often emptied into the hands of small, ragged little boys, nor could he understand how so much wealth should go brushing by, unmindful of the poor."

But dazed or not by the bigness of civilization,

the unevenness of wealth and the general rush of the white man's world, there was one thing which Sitting Bull did not neglect when he came to the land of the Paleface. That was his cunning and his ability to fight.

In the eyes of the Wild West Show he was just an "Injun." To the audience, he might be a strange, fearful creature, to be gawked at, dilated upon, and hated and feared and wondered about as audiences have a habit of doing. But his stardom ceased there. No hurrying flunkeys attended to his wants, no rushing canvasman assisted him with his tepee nor cookhouse waiter brought his meal. When a beef was butchered and the squaws had attended to the niceties of cutting up the animal, Sitting Bull took his apportionment with the rest, hanging up the strips of meat about his tepee, and regarding them as one would regard sudden wealth. When the show arrived in the morning, Sitting Bull put up his own tent, and more than one wandering sightseer, expecting that the conqueror of Custer would be either caged, or at least, partitioned off from ordinary gaze, passed him by without a thought.

It was while he was engaged in the work of setting up his tent one morning in Pittsburgh, that a rather wild-eyed individual hove upon the showgrounds and approached a cowpuncher.

"Where's that damned old renegade?" he asked.

"Just who are yuh referrin' at, Pardner?" asked the cowpuncher and continued to pick his teeth.

"Sitting Bull! Show me the old renegade!" came the announcement in heightened tones, "He killed my brother in that massacre."

The lanky cowboy engineered another difficult manoeuver with his toothpick, then lazily moved into a position into which he could leap to aid in time of trouble. A few feet away, Sitting Bull, giving no evidence whatever that he had heard his name mentioned in a tone of anger, drove vigorously at his pegs, and fussed about the straightening of his tent as though this were all in the world that mattered. The cowpuncher jerked his head.

"Thet's th' ole boy hissef, right there," he said and the avenger rushed forward. He made a speech, to which Sitting Bull paid no attention whatever, contenting himself with slightly heavier blows of the hammer upon those tent pegs. Then with a melodramatic gesture, the stranger swung an arm toward a holster, containing a revolver, and Sitting Bull—without even glancing up—swung his hammer about two feet out of its former line. The blow struck fair. Another avenger of the Custer's Last Fight, had, in the Indian fighting language of the day, bitten the dust. Or perhaps it was the hammer he bit. At any event, when they picked him up, three teeth were missing, and Sitting Bull was still hammering tent stakes.

The Buffalo Bill show prospered more and more now, with the aid of good weather, and the steady augmenting of forces, such as Annie Oakley and Sitting Bull, which appealed to the imaginations of the audiences. For the first time since its beginning, the books of the organization showed a profit when the season ended and Buffalo Bill's Wild West went into winter quarters to prepare for what was to be an auspicious season. Sitting Bull went home, back to the Rosebud, and his old life, his braves and his tepee, content to remain there and view the show business in retrospect, leaving, however, when he went, his bow and sack of finest arrows which he had used more than once in the hunting of deer and buffalo, with Annie Oakley. Sitting Bull rather ran to gifts as far as *Watanya Cicilia* was concerned.

As for "Little Sure Shot," the end of the season meant that she could attend school again, and this she did, hurrying to Cincinnati that she might cram all the learning possible into the few months granted her. This, it may be remarked, at 25, and after a season as the star of what now was a tremendous organization.

Salsbury and Cody had not been idle; with every increasing profit, there had been more additions to the show. The plans for the next year were elaborate; providing as they did for lighting arrangement that would mean night shows, a summer season on Staten Island, New York, and a winter one that was to make history for the organization, an engagement in the old Madison Square Garden, where Annie Oakley would have her first experience of a stellar visit to New York.

One naturally wonders, when Annie Oakley's prowess at shooting is mentioned, what that quality was which caused her to stand out from the herd, and raise what had been a rather mediocre type of performance to one that could hold thousands of persons enthralled. The "Little Missy" was not the first woman who had appeared in public as a rifle expert by any means. In fact, when she married Frank Butler and later became a part of the act of Butler and Oakley, there were at least sixteen women upon the

ANNIE OAKLEY

American stage, all performing tricks of shooting, and all claiming, in the advertisements of
their act, to be the "champion lady rifle shot" of
the world. That was one reason why Annie
Oakley never used the term, or even aspired to
the "feminine championship" even though she
was given the unofficial honor by popular consent. But professionally she refused the title;
there was no such thing as a champion lady rifle
shot of the world for the simple reason that no
contest ever was held to determine one. More
than that, the term had been so misused, even
by the time when Annie Oakley made her first
public appearance, and misused by persons who
could not even shoot, that Annie Oakley rebelled
against it, as being a badge of the faker and
fraud. Miss Oakley's favorite book was one
known as the New Testament. In both private
and public life, she adhered always to its teachings.

The statement has been made that women who
did not know how to shoot called themselves
"the lady rifle champions of the world." Annie
Oakley's notes are authority for this, in one of
her memories she tells of "Winona of the High
Trapeze" who ascended to the rigging at the top
of the tent, and then, swinging by her heels, fired
a rifle at a bullseye whenever her trapeze

reached the limit of its swing. And every time she fired at that metal bullseye, there came the clang of steel, indicating that the bullet had struck dead center.

The act interested Annie Oakley. As far as she could see, that was a pretty good stunt, and one which even she perhaps could not do. So, merely from curiosity in Winona's shooting ability, "Little Missy" invited her one day to a contest, down on the ground where Annie Oakley would have a chance to make a score also. The girl only gasped.

"Oh goodness, Miss Oakley," she exclaimed, "I couldn't do that. Why, I hardly know one end of the gun from the other. I just get up there and pull the trigger, and every time I fire a blank cartridge, a property man pulls a string and rings the bell. That's all I know about shooting!"

In fact, a great many of the "shooting stars" who made their living on the stage at the time of Annie Oakley's debut, knew little more than Winona. There are perhaps more avenues for fakery in stage marksmanship than in perhaps any other types of performance. The Butlers, for instance, attended with some excitement the performance of a stage shot whose main item of interest was his ability to play a piano with a rifle. Above each key was a tiny white disk, which, he explained to the audience, was attached to the hammer which struck the sounding wire of the piano. Therefore, when he fired a bullet and struck this little white disk, the impact threw the hammer against the wire and produced a note. Before him were a number of repeating rifles. At dizzy speed, he explained, he would fire one rifle after another, thus playing a tune.

He began to shoot. Sure enough, the keys of the piano went down every time he pulled the trigger. The tune went on—but suddenly the performer's gun jammed. It so surprised him that he forgot to pick up another, and merely stood there, trying to extricate the offending cartridge. And while he stood impotent, the piano continued to play, on and on and on! The tune had not been produced by rifle bullets whatever, but by a system of invisible wires running to the agile hands of a confederate.

Such were a few of the tricks which existed at that time, and still exist today in many shooting acts, for that matter. The snuffing out of a candle by a rifle bullet was then, and is now, a much simpler thing than it appears. All that is necessary is to hit the board, against which the candle invariably stands, and the swish of the

striking bullet will create enough wind to put
out the flame. The flipping of the ashes of a
cigar held in the mouth of a confederate could
be accomplished even better with a blank cartridge than with a bullet. Bullets are dangerous.
Whereas, with a blank cartridge, all that was
necessary, was to jiggle between the teeth a hair-
pin which ran through the body of the cigar and
the slight movement dropped the ashes without
the aid of a missile whatever.

"For that reason," said Annie Oakley, "whenever I did that trick, I hit the cigar or the cigarette itself, tearing it to pieces with the bullet so
that an audience could be sure that there was no
fakery."

For fakery was rampant—no more perhaps
than it is today—but then there are no Annie
Oakleys today either. The ringing of a bullseye bell by a so-styled champion of the world
was done by a reversal of the usual appearance
of a target. Instead of the bullseye being black,
it was white, surrounded by a large black ring
which could not be seen by the audience. That
ring was of steel—hit any part of an eight inch
target and the bell would ring while the gullible
audience applauded. Then too, there was the
"funnel," a large, black-painted cone of steel
which extended beyond the target. If a bullet

132.

struck within a foot of the desired spot, that funnel could catch it and pull it in to the mark desired—and the bell rang again.

So, it may be seen that there were some really great shots when Annie Oakley entered the field. Persons, for instance, who could place a playing card upon the top of a glass, aim almost without sighting, pull the trigger and knock that playing card off. But the wind did it, not the bullet— the passage of lead within a half a foot would raise the card and drop it to the floor.

Tricks, fakes and more tricks and fakes—yet Annie Oakley not only caused a new interest in shooting, but elevated herself to the position of a star in an organization which, as time went on loaded itself heavily with stellar talent.

The reason that she did it was because she performed, by design, the things which could not be faked.

"It is hard to fake a target that is in the air," Miss Oakley explained in the notations of her memories, "and for that reason I always endeavored to keep things above ground and away from anything where a wire, or an impact could be accused of shattering the object instead of the bullet. When one is shooting at objects in the air, only one thing can be done to aid marksmanship. That is to substitute what is known as mustard seed shot for the bullet in a rifle cartridge. I used this sort of shot to a certain extent in my act, in hitting objects which could not possibly be struck with a rifle bullet, thus making an exceedingly small-bore shotgun out of a rifle. But whenever I did this, I always informed the spectators of the fact—one cannot succeed long when one does not hold the faith of the audience."

It was honesty which helped to make Annie Oakley's shooting the wonderful thing that it was. When the small boy or the grown-up, for that matter, heard the announcer proclaim that Miss Annie Oakley would now attempt to shoot the cigarette out of Mr. Frank Butler's mouth with a single bullet from a .22 calibre rifle, that small boy or that grown-up knew it was to be an actual feat and not a piece of fakery. Faith counts for much.

Faith—and speed, for it was the almost dazzling swiftness with which Annie Oakley did unfakable and seemingly impossible things that caused her to be the favorite, year upon year. Consider for instance, if you ever have attended a day at the traps, the speed with which a clay pigeon leaves its trap, and sails forth to be missed or shattered, as the case may be. Consider then, the speed which one must possess, to stand twenty feet back of one's gun, start with the pulling of the trap, run those twenty feet, pick up the gun, sight, fire and burst that clay target while it still is in the air. That was one of Annie Oakley's feats; later she added to the difficulties by putting two pigeons into the air at once and a table between her and her gun. She must jump over the table, raise her gun and knock down both those targets. The first time she tried it, in public, she fell, shooting from a very undignified sitting position. But she got her targets.

Another event which caused the breath to move a little faster a generation ago was when Annie Oakley, in her buckskin costume and trusty rifle, stepped forth, shot at the thin edge of a playing card held in her husband's hand, and sliced it in two. Or knocked a dime from between his thumb and forefinger at thirty paces. Or hit a swinging ball as it circled about his head at the end of a string. Once, in a contest, with a .22 rifle, she fired 1000 shots at composition balls, thrown into the air. Out of the thousand, she hit fair 943 times, which still remains a mark for other women to shoot at, as Will Rogers would say.

But it was with the shotgun that Annie Oakley caused the thrills to really chase each other along the spectator's spine, and again was this accomplished by the terrific speed and concentration under which she was able to work. One of her stunts was to break six composition balls in four seconds, another being to break five in five seconds, using a rifle for the first shot and finishing up with shotguns, making a change from one gun to another three times in the almost impossible space of time. On occasion, when a real thrill was needed, she could cause six composition balls to be thrown into the air at the same time, and with two shots apiece from three shotguns, burst every one of the targets before they struck the ground.

A hundred other tricks like this were Annie Oakley's, all of them sincere, and since the audience knew the fact, the audience raised her to a point of honor that never has been equalled by any woman of her type. Annie Oakley, in the eyes of the show-spectator of a quarter century or more ago, was the typification of a modern Diana. Newspapers named her that, and spectators gave their approbation. And, by one of her tricks, Annie Oakley achieved a form of notoriety which she did not expect.

The feat was to place a playing card, the ace of hearts, as a target at a distance of twenty-five yards. Then, firing twenty-five shots in twenty-seven seconds, she would obliterate that ace of hearts in the center, leaving only bullet holes in its place. A card thus shot by Annie Oakley formed quite a souvenir in the Eighties.

There came into being a baseball magnate who looked with some disfavor upon passes— as all baseball managers look upon these avenues of free admission. It is the custom, that the doortender may know the ticket to be free, to punch a hole or two in the card, thus saving a miscount when the proceeds of the day were checked. One day a card came to the gate which had been thoroughly perforated. The magnate remarked laconically:

"Huh! Looks like Annie Oakley'd shot at it!"

The remark was repeated—and re-repeated. Soon along Broadway, a new name came into being for a free ticket of admission. It was Annie Oakley, and passes remain Annie Oakleys to this date. The surprising thing being that Annie Oakley herself denied ever having had one of the things.

"I always pay my way," she averred.

Perhaps the greatest feat which Annie Oakley ever performed however, was accomplished the winter before she joined the aggregation headed by Buffalo Bill, and was one which, by necessity, could not be repeated as a part of a regulation performance. That was to fire five thousand rounds, doing the loading herself, all in a day.

Composition balls were used and the place of exhibition was Cincinnati. The effort began in the morning, and lasted for nine hours. On the first thousand, Annie Oakley missed some twenty times. On the second thousand, she missed only sixteen of the composition balls which flew straight from hard-springed traps. Then, tiring, her misses became heavier. But when the nine, gruelling hours were done, she had established a record which, as far as this writer is able to learn, still stands, that of hitting fair on 4,772 flying targets out of a possible five thousand!

Shooting like this may give some idea of the number of times which Annie Oakley pulled the trigger during her eventful lifetime of rifle and shotgun work. It has been estimated that she fired, altogether, not less than two million shots.

In cold figures that does not sound like a terrific amount. But in the hands of a statistician it becomes more formidable. One learns that two million shots would mean a shot every minute, night and day, week after week and month after month for a space of time extending to a continuous total of almost three years! Annie Oakley shot, granting her beginning in this direction, at eight, for fifty-eight years. A third of that time, according to the usual order of things, was spent in sleep. That leaves thirty-nine. Pursuing the statistician farther, one finds, now that the reduction has become complete, one thirteenth of Annie Oakley's waking life was spent in pulling the trigger.

Chapter Eight

WHEN one depicts the history of Annie Oakley, there by necessity arises also the depiction of the early history of that most American of institutions, the Buffalo Bill Wild West. The two were so intermingled, so inter-dependent that one is not complete without the other—the Wild West was not really wild without the addition of the Ohio girl who so easily was mistaken for an important personage from the far away plains, and Annie Oakley herself did not reach her pinnacle until she had gained for a background the cowboys, the Indians and vaqueros who formed the exhibition captained by Buffalo Bill.

The season of 1886 began according to the exciting plans which had been made for it—a summer on Staten Island and after that, an indoor exhibition for the first time in its history at Madison Square Garden. Naturally, those engagements were the subject of every conversation, of every plan; performers saved when they might have spent, that there would be money for new costumes and accoutrements; Buffalo Bill's show was coming into its own at last.

ANNIE OAKLEY

Not the least of those who planned was Annie Oakley. Staten Island was about the biggest place in the world just then; she sewed on new costumes, she bought new trappings for her horse. Staten Island and the big parade that would be given in New York on the day of the opening! Those things are vital to a performer.

The show began its season in St. Louis, gradually working East, that it might arrive at its New York engagement at the height of the summer. All went well until Washington; then as she worked in the arena, Annie Oakley felt a queer sensation in one ear, followed by a buzzing and scrambling. A small bug had penetrated the orifice and, try as she would between shots, she could not dislodge it.

The act was on and that was all that counted. For a time she forgot the pain, only to have it recur tenfold once her shooting was over and she had gone to her dressing tent. Someone about the show suggested sweet oil and it was applied, but to no purpose. Then a visit was made to a physician. An examination convinced him that the bug had departed—but it was still there.

A week of agony followed, in which the ear continued to swell, accompanied by terrific headaches. The time came when Annie Oakley

could not even rest her head upon a pillow—
sleep had vanished; she spent her resting hours
upright in a steamer chair with applications to
her ear; but when the time for her act arrived,
she ran into the arena as usual; the audience
knew nothing but that health and strength and
easy rest were hers continually.

The necessity for a performance can arouse
superhuman traits in an actor. The old adage
that "the show must go on" has traveled through
too many generations to be denied for anything
short of absolute incapacity. So it was with
Annie Oakley. She performed her feats of
marksmanship while the arena swam about her
and when she actually staggered to her dressing
tent, once the concentration of effort induced by
the sight of the audience had passed. It only
resulted in more agony, accompanied by constant
administrations of warm water and castile soap
—Annie hadn't believed the doctor, and at last
there came confirmation of her opinion. The
invader, very dead, came forth, but he had left
a souvenir of his visit.

It was an abscess which continued to increase
in viciousness until Annie Oakley at last performed her act while suffering from a temperature which hovered at the danger stage. Doctors had been evaded; performers often do that

as they take the fighting chance that they will survive a malady and be able to continue their act, whereas a doctor might order them to bed and see that they went there. In addition to being a true performer, Annie Oakley possessed more grit than ordinary; in vain did her husband, Buffalo Bill and others argue with her. Everything would be all right on the morrow. But when the morrow came, there was only increased inflammation and suffering. At last came the day when the troupe assembled for its transferral upon a chartered ferry-boat to New York City for the parade—one incidentally which was to consume seventeen miles of horseback travel. It was the thing for which Annie Oakley had hoped and dreamed—and at seventhirty that morning the crack shot had received her orders from a physician. There would be no parade for her. Instead, with every attempt at rest, she was to place leeches upon that ear— they were considered an infallible remedy for inflammation in those days—and remain quiet.

From her tent, Annie Oakley watched the parade ride away, down to the landing for the trip to New York. Her husband, Buffalo Bill, Nate Salsbury, all had gone. She, of all the performers, was left alone upon the exhibition grounds, the only remainder of the show save the few attendants, workingmen and hostlers. The sound of hoofbeats faded, while Annie Oakley sat and looked at a bottle containing two leeches, glancing meanwhile at the costume, bought for that parade, the horse trappings with the name "Oakley" in gold letters upon them— useless now because of an investigative bug. Minute after minute the suffering woman struggled against temptation, and failed. A hostler passed, she called him to the tent.

"Bring my horse here at once!" she ordered. "Put these vocaroes on him. I'm going in that parade."

The tent flap dropped, and from behind it came the sounds of excited scurrying; Annie Oakley was putting on that beloved costume. The horse arrived, the tent-flap opened. Annie Oakley leaped to her saddle, headache, earache, inflammation and all and galloped through the side of the exhibition grounds on the trail of that parade.

She caught the boat just as the last of the paraphernalia was being loaded, and then, dismounting with the cheery announcement that she had simply felt so much better that it would have been a shame not to have accompanied the parade, she rested until the New York side was reached. Then into the saddle again, and to seventeen miles of smiles and band-music. But when the boat was reached again, Frank Butler, with a cry of concern, ran hurriedly to his wife. She had collapsed in the saddle. They called the doctor again when Staten Island was reached; in the little tent an operation was performed which usually required the services of a hospital and operating room; that delicate task of lancing beyond an eardrum, while vaguely through the haze—for there had been no anaesthetic, Annie Oakley heard the surgeon announce that blood poisoning had developed and that she had one chance out of twelve for recovery.

"All right," she muttered against the pain, "that'll be a fighting chance."

Swiftly the word traveled around the exhibition grounds—that Annie Oakley was fighting for her life. The show opened to a packed house, many of whom were there to see the widely known girl shot. A harassed management, fighting for time, decided upon an announcement that the little star had met with an accident, but that she would be able to again appear in a week, planning at the end of that time to announce another week's disability and thus continue the postponements until the matter was settled, for life or for death. But in exactly four days, a young woman, her eyes so swollen that she could barely see, her walk a mixture of dragging step and directionless stagger, her head bandaged, moved into the arena, leaned against the table which supported her guns, shot her complete act and moved wanly out again. Annie Oakley had won her fight for life; it was the first and last time that she missed a performance during her whole engagement with the Buffalo Bill Wild West.

Of such are the difficulties of one who lives because of that vague, uncertain thing known as an audience. But then, the life of a performer with the Buffalo Bill show in its embryo days was fairly certain of difficulties of one kind or another almost constantly. It was by difficulties that the show grew, sometimes of a serious nature, such as the winter following the Staten Island engagement, when the show entered Madison Square Garden for its first engagement under shelter, and when the ravages of winter and pneumonia descended upon the buffalo, killing them off until only one was left, to the more ludicrous events, caused by attempts, while still in the open, to give that wonder of wonders in those days, a night show.

Lamps and gas flares were devised and set about the grounds, so that the audience—what

of it that came following the first few performances—could at least gain a shadowy glimpse
of the actors as they came and went, and the
flights of the bucking horse riders as, yielding
now and then to the superiority of their mounts,
they careened through the air to the earthy
cushion of the arena. Red fire aided the Indians
in their dancing, and lent an especially vivid
atmosphere to the attack on the old Deadwood
Stagecoach. But the one thing upon which the
show thrived more than any other, had suffered
severely. That was the shooting.

"How's anybody going to enjoy this show?"
asked Buffalo Bill, "When they can't see th'
shootin', and when th' shooters can't see what
they're shootin' at? Some of you fellows around
here rig up something. Annie and myself can't
see those clay pigeons five feet off in this light.
Let's get it fixed."

Whereupon the every Edison of the company
went into conference. A hundred schemes were
devised, none of which seemed practical. But
at last, one of the members winked heavily, indicating a great idea, and disappeared, in the direction of town and purchases. That night,
when the first trap was released, a spurt of blue
flame traveled outward, to die with the pulling

of the trigger of the gun in the hands of Annie Oakley. Buffalo Bill stroked his goatee.

"Looks like that's goin' to work fine," he said. But a moment later, he recanted. The idea had taken the shape of wads of cotton, soaked with alcohol and glued to the clay pigeons. These wads were lighted an instant before the release of the trap, and were destined to make a sailing circle of light through the air at which to shoot. But when Buffalo Bill's turn came, something was wrong. The wad of light dropped about three feet from the trap, while a vague missile went traveling on. The glue had failed to hold, as it failed time after time. The great idea went into the discard.

"If you can't get anything better than that, better give it up," grunted Cody. The inventor beamed.

"Oh, I'll have it by tomorrow night," he said. "The idea just came to me."

The next night, Annie Oakley stepped to her trap.

"Pull!" she called and a circle of light shot forth. A quick aim, a steady pull on the trigger —and the circle of light continued to travel.

"Missed!" called the announcer. Annie Oakley set herself for a second shot.

"Pull!" she commanded.

"Missed!" came the cry from the scorer as another beaming circle of light traveled on untarnished.

"Pull!" snapped Annie Oakley with a bit of temper in her tone. She aimed this time to annihilate the clay pigeon with its beacon light. But the cry was again:

"Missed!"

So it was on through the total of ten shots. Then came Buffalo Bill, the Indian Slayer, he who at many a pace had shot the horse from beneath Yellowhand as the pair advanced to the great duel at the Battle of the Warbonnet, Cody the dead-shot, Old Never-miss Himself.

"Pull!" he commanded and the trap-puller pulled. Out shot the gleaming parabola.

"Missed!" said the announcer with something of awe in his tone. About this time a heavy titter began in the grandstand. Cody scowled at his shotgun.

"Wonder what's wrong with this danged thing?" he asked. Then: "Pull!"

"Missed!" It was becoming very monotonous by this time. Colonel William Frederick Cody reached for another gun.

"Pull!" he bellowed.

It was the same old thing. The grandstand was roaring now. Again Cody gave the command, again the monotonous reply announced that he had failed to score a target. Again and again and again and again—the whole set of ten were gone through, all with the same result. Bat eyed with chagrin, Buffalo Bill and Annie Oakley made a pretense of bowing to the audience, and then, happy in the arrival of other events, let the show go on. But something about those twenty consecutive misses aroused their curiosity.

"Oh, there ain't any doubt about us missing 'em," said Buffalo Bill, as in the semi-darkness after the show, the pair went forth to the scene of their terrific defeat and hunted about for the clay pigeons, "I could see 'em sailing off, just as plain as day. Ain't it funny now, we didn't hit a one of 'em?"

"Didn't we?" asked Annie Oakley as she picked up one of the hateful targets, only to have it disintegrate in her hands. "Then why did this break so easily? And what—."

That was it. The thing which sent Buffalo Bill in roaring search of a would-be inventor— who would, however, not invent again. Since the cotton had not stuck to the clay pigeons by the mere application of mucilage, the Wild West Edison had determined upon more drastic means. He therefore had hied himself to a drugstore, and there purchased large amounts of

150.

sticking plaster, such as once glued itself to the skins of unfortunates suffering from a "crick" in the back. This he had cut into strips and, in order that the cotton might be held in place, so crisscrossed the clay pigeons with the adhesive, that it had been next to impossible to shatter them.

One by one the two surprised crack-shots examined the targets which cluttered the grounds. In every one of them were tiny holes, indicating a puncture by shot, and which, under ordinary circumstances, would have broken the pigeons. But the sticking plaster had held true to its task, and held also those clay pigeons from breaking. A roaring Buffalo Bill sought out the inventor, and spoke his mind—which, to those who knew Buffalo Bill—was of no uncertain quality when things went amiss about the Wild West. After that, self-illuminated clay pigeons were deleted as a part of the performance.

Annie Oakley now was no longer the only white woman with the Buffalo Bill troupe. More women had been added, some of them riders, others crack shots who trailed in the wake of the Darke County expert, and still more merely "cowgirls" and "lassies of the plains" who did little more than make their appearance in buckskin dresses and big hats and lend variety to the scene. The show prospered on Staten Island, to an extent that had not been believed possible, and after its extremely successful season closed for a short time that it might make ready for its appearance in Madison Square Garden. During this intermission, Annie Oakley learned that fortitude must be hers, either in or out of the arena.

It had become the practise of Frank Butler, as her manager, to keep her before the public as much as possible in a legitimate shooting atmosphere, to say nothing of the money involved. With this plan, contests were continually being arranged, at which Annie Oakley shot against some of the best male wing and trap experts of the country, the emolument often being a share of the gate receipts received by the gun club where the contest was held.

This particular contest was to be against an English champion, the winner to be the one scoring best on fifty birds. It was rather an important shoot, and the morning before the match, Annie Oakley decided to practise on twenty-five targets with a new gun which she had hoped to use in the contest. She made ready, and had proferred her gun to her husband for a first shot, herself arranging the trap. As she slid in the target and was withdrawing her hand, the spiral spring which was then used to throw the birds, flew from its fastenings, and released the trap.

Out sprang an angry tongue of metal, striking between the first and second fingers of Annie Oakley's left hand, cutting between the bones and literally splitting the member for a depth of two and a half inches. The woman paled, swung dizzily, then with the tremendous recuperative power which was a part of her nature, straightened.

"I suppose we'd better give it up for today, Frank," she said with as little concern as possible. "Perhaps, if I'm going to use this hand tomorrow, I'd better see a doctor."

The guess was confirmed when the badly lacerated hand was released from its bandages in the office of the surgeon. When his work was finished, fourteen inches of catgut had been necessary, in deep, agonizing stitches which ran almost directly through the woman's hand, to hold the raw edges of the wound together. This was followed by the command that the injured hand should not be used for at least two weeks.

"But that's impossible, Doctor," said Annie Oakley, "I am booked to shoot a match tomorrow."

"Match or no match, that hand must not be

used. The slightest effort will break those stitches. Then the wound may require months to heal."

Annie Oakley arose the next morning, obdurate. At least, she told her husband, they would make their appearance at the shooting grounds. This was done, whereupon Frank Butler made an earnest effort to have the match postponed. The rival shot and his manager went into conference. Through an open window, Annie Oakley heard the following conversation.

"No, I tell you, we won't postpone it. The match is won and the money is ours. She can't shoot with that hand in a sling—we've won the match."

"Have they?" asked Miss Oakley, belligerency rising over caution. "Frank, you just go ahead and make the arrangements. I'll shoot against him."

"But you can't. That hand—."

"I'll shoot with one hand before I'll submit to anything like that!" answered the diminuitive crack shot. This, of course, appended by the feminine: "The idea!"

By this time, attendants of the gun club were stretching ropes to hold back a crowd which now threatened to overflow the grounds. Frank Butler, yielding to the determination of his wife,

A famous painting from a photograph of Miss Oakley in action.

stepped forward, made an anouncement concerning the accident of the day previous and added:

"Miss Oakley will attempt to shoot with one hand against her competitor. If, at any time she decides to discontinue the match, she will be glad to refund to the spectators the seventy-five per cent of the gate receipts which is to go to her as her share. Or, if anyone at this time, cares to get their full admission price back, it can be arranged by applying at the gate."

No one left. The idea of watching a woman shoot with one hand against a champion using both hands was worth watching. The match began and Miss Oakley, winning the toss, went first to the traps. A bird rose and a bird fell; Miss Oakley had grassed her first target and a cheer greeted her one-handed effort. Then the champion went to the trap and he too scored. Time after time they shot, each holding even, the champion working his hardest with both hands, the woman raising her shotgun with her right, sighting it and pulling the trigger, while her left hand, sure support of a shotgun, especially at the traps, remained inactive in its bandages. To the eleventh bird they traveled, with the score tied. Then from the trap came a streak of lightning in the shape of a bird, rising high on the left quarter, so swiftly in fact that

ANNIE OAKLEY

Annie Oakley could not raise her gun in time to send it the full charge of shot. The tail feathers flew from the quarry with the striking of the load, but the bird went on, heading swiftly for the back boundary.

The gun was too heavy to be sighted swiftly for another shot; it was a case of risking that injured hand or losing a bird—and Annie Oakley thought more of her score than of pain. A swift pull and she had jerked her lacerated hand from its sling and thrown it into position to support her gun. A swifter sighting, a quick pull of the trigger and then with a little groan, Annie Oakley stood impotent, vainly attempting to hide the sight of spurting blood from the spectators. The swift movement to the gun barrel, accompanied by the impact of explosion, had torn more than half the stitches from their fastenings; an injury had been made even worse now. But that was not the reason why Annie Oakley had groaned. Her effort had been for naught; the bird had dropped dead only six inches out of bounds.

Meanwhile Frank Butler had leaped to the table upon which the referee had been scoring and called off the match. The champion stepped forward for his eleventh shot and missed with both barrels, thus making the score, so far at

156.

least, a draw. When the crowd had melted away, and the pair prepared to seek anew the services of a surgeon, Frank Butler said concernedly:

"I just knew you'd hurt your hand again, Annie."

"Oh well," she answered, with a quick smile, "we didn't disappoint the audience anyway. Nobody asked for their money back."

The audience—always the audience. Despite the second accident, Annie Oakley, two weeks later, entered a three heat riding race at a fair at which she had been booked, and which she felt would be unfair to cancel, to say nothing of giving an exhibition of shooting from horseback. Incidentally, she won the race. After that, however, she used more discretion. Time was drawing near for the opening of the Buffalo Bill show in Madison Square Garden, and when that time came, rest and care had made a shooting hand whole again.

A blatant winter season followed, the beginning of many that were to be played by Buffalo Bill and his Congress of Rough Riders in the historic old building of Madison Square Garden. Then, at the close of the season, Annie Oakley hurried back to Ohio for an important visit.

Two of her sisters had died, victims of that scourge which seemed particularly deadly in the Mozee family, tuberculosis. Joseph Shaw, the third husband, had suffered from the hand of misfortune which had struck two others before him; now he was blind and destined soon to die. Annie Oakley told him farewell; she knew that she would not see him again. For "Little Missy" was going into far lands, upon the quest of great adventure.

Chapter Nine

THE old Madison Square Garden had formed a great field of endeavor for Messrs. Cody and Salsbury, and there the show often had played to attendances as high as thirty thousand persons in a single day. The New York papers had been filled with the achievements of the organization, new stunts had been added, Annie Oakley had essayed wild west riding of the type known as "trick ridin'" but with a sidesaddle instead of the safer astride saddle which is used today, and the show had practically doubled in size and performance since its wandering days. It was therefore not unusual that when a group of American capitalists decided to venture their money upon an exhibition of American products in England that they should seek the aid of the two western showmen to furnish the amusement.

The exhibition labored under the topheavy title of "An Exhibition of The Arts, Industries, Manufactures, Products and Resources of the United States," which happily was shortened by common usage to "The American Exhibition." It was to continue for some two months in England, and the Buffalo Bill Show, if it would take the journey, would be entitled to a percentage of the entire gate receipts. It was a rather fortunate idea on the part of the promoters; from the yellowed clippings which remain as testimony to the Exhibition of Arts, Industries and other things, one gains the opinion that the British Isles could have existed wonderfully well without a glimpse at any of them. But England did care about the Wild West, and thereby hang many tales.

Preparations now were made for making the show even greater; the addition of more crack shots, the augmenting of the Indian contingent until it included more than a hundred representatives of the Sioux, Cheyenne, Kiowa, Pawnee and Ogalalla tribes, while among the chieftains was Red Shirt, a redoubtable warrior on his own home grounds, and second only in power to Sitting Bull himself. There were more cowboys, and the first Cowboy Band, Mexican wild riders, buffalo, Texas steers, burros, bronchos, racing horses, elk, bears and numerous other attractions in numbers sufficient that when the problem of transportation arose, the promoters found that it could be solved only by the chartering of an entire steamer.

Thus, on March 31, 1887, while the Cowboy

ANNIE OAKLEY

Band played "The Girl I Left Behind Me"—
a rather appropriate number if the adulation
given the modern rodeo hand at a New York
exhibition forms any criterion for other exhibits
of the past—the good ship State of Nebraska
set sail for England, loaded with everything
from tents to Indians, who, according to the tradition of their tribes, would proceed at once to
melt away to skin and bones and then depart
soulless into a new world where there could be
no happy hunting grounds because of the water.
The tradition increased to a certainty about the
time the ship began to roll. Even Red Shirt,
whose main reputation had been gained by walking into the camp of a rival who strove to steal
his chieftainship, and thoroughly killing that
Indian insurrectionist before the eyes of his wife,
admitted that there was a good deal to the super-
stition, and that he felt reasonably sure he was
about to die. Never perhaps had there been a
more disconsolate band of Indians.

As for Annie Oakley, she had speedily made
the acquaintance of the captain and been given
the right to the bridge. It was here she stood
one day—one who reviews the history of Annie
Oakley would expect nothing else—when the
smash of a storm rolled down upon the ship,
lashing it in the crash of waves and the roll of

ANNIE OAKLEY

billow until Miss Oakley decided that perhaps
she had better go below. But she was halted
even as she started; the descent was too dangerous. Then came the news; the Buffalo Bill
Wild West was adrift and helpless, upon a ship
with an injured propellor, and every hour bringing more damage to the boat. For forty-eight
hours the State of Nebraska drifted helpless in
the trough of the sea, while below Indians feared
to die and likewise feared they wouldn't, the
hard riding, hard shooting Buffalo Bill wobbled
weakly about, sick, as he expressed it, as a cow
critter with hollow-horn, horses jammed against
each other in the holds, buffalo strove to stam-
pede, hollow-eyed cowpunchers wished for the
broad prairee once more, and the Buffalo Bill
Wild West faced extinction.

"Ten of those forty-eight hours" Annie Oakley noted, "I spent wrapped in a seafaring oil-
skin with head protected by a sou'wester,
strapped securely on the captain's deck. Just
why I was allowed there, I never knew, but I
learned the power of the mighty waves. It was
a glorious sight, our boat being dashed from side
to side; I felt that one foot further and we would
be turned bottom-side up. For forty-eight hours,
the old, grizzled Scotch captain never left the
deck. Double watches were placed on every

162.

post. Before I left the bridge the word came up: 'All ready!' meaning that the necessary repairs to the propellor had been made, and the boat executed a dangerous turn and headed toward England. We had drifted two hundred and forty-six miles out of our course. Not a passenger, except my husband and myself, knew the true danger we all had been in."

Foggy England was doubly-welcomed after that; two weeks of rehearsals and the show opened at what was known as Earl's Court, purporting to give what the programs called "America's National Entertainment" and the protracted engagement which saved the life of the American Exhibition was on.

A year or so ago, this writer had opportunity to gauge just how literally London took that subtitle of "America's National Entertainment." A rare thing had happened, a sunshiny day in London, and I strolled past Picadilly Circus, up a narrow lane of a street, then off at another angle, finally to find myself in what might have been called a square had it not been so multi-angular. Across one of the slanting streets, I saw a boarding stable, and before it something which caused me, from the West, to look closer. Then I started forward, hurriedly. The first glance had been correct; the exhibit was a collection of

some hundred "ropin' saddles," such as the kind
one sees upon the ranches of Colorado, Wyo-
ming and Montana. Rather amazing that such
things should find a resting place within ten
minutes walk of Picadilly and the Strand.

Yet they were the true saddles; here was one
bearing the stamp of a saddle-maker in Fort
Worth, Texas. Another came from Pueblo,
Colorado, still others from Miles City, Montana, Salt Lake City and other towns of the
West. Amazed, I sought the Cockney owner and
made inquiries.

"O, Buffalo Bill 'e started hit," he said. " 'E
kime over 'ere with 'is show and the swells took
'im up, y'know. Then they must ride like the
Hummericans. Well, hit rawther started a fad,
do you call it? We've 'ad a trade in the bloody
things ever since."

Buffalo Bill invaded England forty years ago.
That a fad started by him should exist, even in a
small sense, that length of time, is evidence
enough of the furore which his show created.

Yet the invasion of "America's National Entertainment" found England, at first, decidedly
cagey regarding both the Exposition and the
amusement enterprise which had been brought
along to furnish the diversions. There was, to
a large extent, a certain amount of anti-Yankee

feeling, together with a total lack of understanding what all this shouting of savages and bluster of cowboys was about.

True, the arrival awakened interest, and the speed with which the show worked, as it arrived in London, traveled some twelve miles to the grounds, set up tents, equipment, reorganized after the long journey across the sea, the landing at Gravesend and the travel by train into London, put up the cook-tents, levelled the ground, staked out the arena and put the show into shape for the beginning of rehearsals the next day, all in less than ten hours. Copious articles were printed in the various papers about "Yankee ingenuity" and American speed, but when the performance came, there was at times at least, a noticeable animosity in many quarters. A part of this was due to a natural antipathy, still more was caused by the fact that the show as such, greatly augmented since its last appearance in America, was topheavy and poorly generalled, the acts not yet having been put in their proper sphere. But a great part of it was caused by the fact that the English did not understand. Indians were to them far away things. Cowboys, to the literal English mind, would not ride on really wild horses of their own accord; certainly they must be trained to these things and very tame when not working in the ring. And so it went. But there was one act that they did grasp and that was the work of Annie Oakley. If one is to judge by the aged clippings describing the beginnings of Buffalo Bill's sojourn in London, one inevitably comes to the conclusion that the little "western" from Darke County, Ohio played an exceptionally heavy role in maintaining the wave of popularity which became the lot of Cody and Salsbury.

"It was a relief when Annie Oakley appeared," said one of the most powerful critics. "Somehow, the vast audience expected to see something and they were not disappointed, for she shattered the flying missiles with precision and dramatic effect."

Thus ran many of the reviews, while the rest of them, in the main complimentary, indicated that the failure of the Buffalo Bill Wild West would please at least a few. To wit:

"Went Buffalo Billing at the American Exhibition. One could hardly mistake the nationality of the majority of the audience. The enormous headgear worn by the women would betray them as Yankees anywhere.

"An overgrown circus seems an awkward remark to make of the entertainment our American cousins are providing us with, but despite the fact that being

Jubilee year, and that naturally we are loving every nation and everybody, and also despite Canon Farrar's prayer, Buffalo Bill's exhibition is neither more nor less than a hippodrome on an enormous scale. All the best of it we have seen before, either at Covent Garden or at Olympia."

How different from a later review, when public sentiment had, as if by a miracle, undergone a wonderful change and, the Buffalo Bill show was the most talked of thing in London! For here is a vastly variant viewpoint:

"Saving for Buffalo Bill's show, the American Exhibition is a ghastly failure. It is all very well to say that it is not complete yet, neither was the Colonial and Indian Exhibition last year at the outset, but what a difference from the present ill-sorted congeries of uninteresting trifles...........From the Fair Trade point of view it is satisfactory to find that this introduction of American products, free of duty into our country is not likely in any way to damage our home markets—the products are, in homely phrase, not good enough.

"Far different must be our report of Buffalo Bill, who is a grand success. On Monday, the audience which crowded the vast ampitheater, with its 20,000 seats, was thoroughly representative. Glancing at the boxes, we noticed one in the possession of Lady Rudolph Churchill and party; a regular Savoy box contained Messrs. Gilbert and Sullivan, and D'Oyly Carte; while Mr. Charles Wyndham and his following occupied another. Messrs. Toole and Thorne occupied another; on all sides familiar faces were visible: Mr. Augustus Harris, Mr. Oscar Wilde, Miss Marie Linden, Miss Emily Thorne, Mr. Hughie Drummond, Colonel Hughes Hallett and innumerable others."

These were all important names in London in 1887, the year of Queen Victoria's Jubilee. And it had been these names and others of greater and lesser degree which had sent a tidal wave of popularity surging in the direction of Colonel William Frederick Cody and his show, of which Annie Oakley formed an important part.

The first adherence had been largely American—"Yankees" attending an exhibition from their home country. Then gradually that strata known as Society had become interested in the portrayals of Indian massacres, cowboy amusements, western shooting events and whatnot. The fancy soon had become a fad, and while the lesser trailed in the wake of the great and the dollars tinkled into the till of the firm of Cody and Salsbury those who would have gladly seen the Yankee Buffalo Bill fail ignominiously, yawped and chattered without avail. But they continued nevertheless in a manner best indicated by the following remarks from a London "comment" column of 1887:

168.

ANNIE OAKLEY

"The Buffalo Bill furore is becoming ridiculous. Colonel Cody is, no doubt, an eminent man in his way, and for bossing a show even the great Barnum in his best days could not surpass him. But are these credentials sufficient to justify an outburst of fashionable fetish worship? London society should remember the shame which fell upon it for its adoration of that black miscreant, Cetowayo. On the whole, I cannot but consider it a mistake for Lord Beresford to have given the Yankee showman a mount on the box seat of his drag at the Coaching Club meet. *Noblesse oblige,* there is a want of congruity in the companionship of an illustrious officer who fills an important position in the Government with a gentleman chiefly famed as an adroit scalper of Red Indians. I do not blame Buffalo Bill; my censure is confined to the fashionable throng who pay their devotion at such a shrine."

From that may be seen the thoroughly hearty welcome which a great part of the rank and file of England was willing to extend to the man who, in this country, is not looked upon as much as an adroit scalper of Indians as a builder of the tremendous West and its civilization. And when Buffalo Bill was mentioned in this tempo, the same went for all the rest of the show in greater or lesser degree. But, strange to say, it only increased the popularity of the performers; at this time Annie Oakley was receiving literally tons of flowers from those who had admired her

work in the arena and who had met her following the performances; it became a part of her
daily duties when, four times a day, the heavy
laden Parcel Post came in, to sort out the gifts of
the upper strata of London, then send them on
their way anew, that they might perform a more
humane duty in London hospitals than that of
withering upon an exhibition grounds.

Society—London society—was demonstrating
that perhaps the snobbery accredited it existed
more in the classes which strove to ape it, than
in its own ranks. More and more the vitriolic
pens of lampoonists and columnists of the day
commented upon the "furore," but even as the
jibes were printed, the solemn society columns
of the same papers bore an increasingly long list
of notables who had attended the performances
of the adroit scalper, Little Sure Shot and the
rest of the American aggregation. But there
was one portal at which the scribes were forced
to halt. That was the door of royalty.

The Prince of Wales, later King Edward of
England, loved the outdoors, its sports and its
activities. Even before the Wild West buildings
were finished, while the track was incomplete
and while arrangements were still in a somewhat
chaotic state, he had sent a communication from
Marlborough House that had resulted in a

170.

Another bit of daring, which helped to draw the crowds to the big tent.

special performance for the Prince and Princess and their party, consisting of their three daughters, the Princesses Louise, Victoria and Maude; the Marquis of Lorne and Princess Louise, his wife, the Duke of Cambridge, the Comptesse de Paris, the Crown Prince of Denmark and numerous lords and ladies in waiting. It was this visit which had given to society its real impetus, and it was to be followed by more examples of royal support that would end forever the common run of objection to the invasion of the "Yankee" show and do much to wipe out what was but poorly veiled American antipathy of a most heightened character. No one ever has given either Buffalo Bill or Annie Oakley the political dignity of being ambassadors to foreign lands. Yet, when one reads the press comments of English papers at the beginning of the Buffalo Bill show in London, and follows those same papers through to the time when the Wild West departed, one may easily see that something more than an exhibition of western antics was given at Earl's Court. A communion was established between England and America which wiped out many false ideas, and resulted in a general feeling of friendship that has grown steadily to this day. And, unofficially, of course, there was even more of a diplomatic character to one incident in which Annie Oakley played far more of a leading part than she knew.

In spite of the unfinished condition of affairs, Buffalo Bill had determined that the show should be given for the Prince and Princess on the day specified. The Royal Party arrived. The grand entree was made, other various events run through, and at last Annie Oakley came forth to shoot.

The act made an instantaneous hit with the Royal Party, with the result that a request went forth that the young lady of the unerring aim be presented to the Prince and Princess. She went forward—but the story is best told in the naive notes of Annie Oakley herself:

"As the last gun I had used lay on the table, still smoking with the heat, the Prince of Wales, who with Alexandria, occupied the lower center box, asked if I might be presented. Our orator, Frank Richmond, who stood at a corner of their box, gave a slight inclination of his head as I bowed to them. I went into the box. What a fine looking, college-bred man our Frank Richmond was! His presentation speech was: 'Your Royal Highnesses, I have the honor to present Annie Oakley.'

"I had heard a great deal about how women tried to flirt with the Prince while the gentle Princess held her peace and now it all ran before me. An English born lady would not have dared to have done as I did—they must speak to Royalty according to the station of the Royal personages. The Prince's hand came over the low front of the box as they all rose to their feet. I ignored it and quickly proffered my hand to his Princess. She did not offer the tips of her fingers, expecting me to kneel and kiss them, but took my hand gently in her own, saying: 'What a wonderful little girl.' Nor was His Highness displeased at what I had dared to do, for he too, shook my hand warmly when I turned from the Princess to him, and after I had bowed far enough to turn my back, he made this remark, loud enough for the whole assembly to hear: 'What a pity there are not more women in the world like that little one!' "

But evidently Annie Oakley didn't explain all this at the time to Colonel William Frederick Cody, for in his memoirs, there is a widely different version of the affair:

"Our lady shot expert, on being presented at the finish, committed the little mistake of offering to shake hands with the Princess, for, be it known, feminine royalty offers the hand back uppermost which the person presented is expected to lift with fingertips and salute with the lips. However, the Princess was quick to perceive, and she solved the situation by taking the proffered hand, somewhat shaded with gunpowder and shaking it heartily."

Which displays after all that everything lies in the viewpoint. But be that as it may, Prince

Edward was evidently far from displeased. It was not long afterward that, early one morning, a message arrived in camp. It read:

"Colonel William Frederick Cody,
Dear Sir:
Will the little girl, Annie Oakley, who shoots so cleverly in your show, object to shooting a friendly match with the Grand Duke Michael of Russia? We will arrive at Earl's Court at 10:30 this morning.

Edward."

There was nothing to do but accept. The future King of England had commanded Little Sure Shot to an international match. Nor did either of them know that the command might also lead—to the breaking of one!

Chapter Ten

THE request of the Prince of Wales brought consternation—and much argument to the camp of the Buffalo Bill Wild West.

"Go on!" said Nate Salsbury, "you can beat him."

"Hold on there!" Buffalo Bill broke in, "there's just the hitch. She shouldn't beat the Grand Duke. That'd be terrible."

Thus the argument went on; Cody, the showman, believing that one should do the proper thing at all times—especially when a Grand Duke of Russia believed himself a good shot. But Annie Oakley and her husband had a different idea.

"If what we hear of him is true," said Miss Oakley, "I won't have to let him beat me. I'll have to do my best shooting to even tie him."

"Shoot him off his feet!" said Nate Salsbury, while the be-whiskered Major Burke, press agent extraordinary, all but wept. To be so unkind to royalty!

The conference at last was over, and Frank

Butler and his wife went into the arena where the contest was to be held. There they made use of a little private information. The Grand Duke bore the reputation of being one of the best shots in Russia. But from what Annie Oakley and her husband had heard of him, he got his best results on clay birds which flew about forty yards from the trap, a slower flight than Annie Oakley prepared for him on that day of their private match.

"We'll just make it a good test," she said, and ordered the traps screwed down to sixty-five yards. "That'll be something to shoot at."

Promptly at 10:30 o'clock, according to Annie Oakley's recital, four carriages rolled into the Wild West grounds. They contained Edward, The Prince of Wales, Alexandra, the Princess of Wales, the Duke of Clarence, George, now King of England, the Grand Duke Michael of Russia and his suite, the Princess Louise, the Princess Maude and one very important personage in the eyes of the Grand Duke Michael, the Princess Victoria of England, daughter of the Prince of Wales. Much had been printed regarding the Grand Duke and the Princess Victoria. The English papers had not been at all hesitant about stating that Michael was in England upon a special mission, that of uniting the two countries by persuading a marriage in which the Princess Victoria and himself were to be the principals. Some opposed the marriage; others were in favor of it.

The contest began, the winner to be judged by the best score out of fifty targets, while the Royal party assembled in the boxes to watch the battle. Or what had been meant for one.

Because, after all, it wasn't. By the time the first ten targets had been sprung, Annie Oakley had moved into the lead. When thirty had been reached, the Grand Duke Michael was fighting hard, but with a handicap which seemed impossible to overcome. And when the end of the match arrived, it brought a result by which Annie Oakley had missed only three targets out of fifty, while the Grand Duke of Russia had failed on fourteen.

Then began a perfect torrent of lampooning in those papers unfavorable to the Grand Duke's alleged mission. Shooting had been Michael's hobby, and one of his claims to fame—other, of course, than that of occupying the position of importance which he held in Russia. He had failed, in a match of his own seeking, and the fact gave to those conducting the campaign of publicity against him, a weapon by which to thrust and jibe and jeer, as is evidenced by the

following from the Evening News and Tele-
phone of London, shortly following the event:

"Fame, but not notoriety, is silent about this
noble scion of Russia, who is said to have visited
this country, not alone for the purpose of attending
Her Majesty's Jubilee, but to find a wife from
among the daughters of The Prince of Wales.
Whatever may be the faults of the Grand Duke,
and reports say that they are very many, he must
be credited with a great love of sport of all kinds,
and in his own country he is a great and generous
patron of everything connected with sport. Only a
day or two ago he asked to be allowed to enter into
competition with Miss Annie Oakley at the Wild
West Show at Earl's Court, which permission was
at once accorded. But although the Grand Duke
made a fairly good score, it showed but poorly
in comparison with that of his fair competitor, and
he retired from the contest abashed, but firmly convinced of the superiority of American markswomen
over Russian amateur lady-shots."

As for the rest of the unfavorable lampoonists:

"It was the most amazing and unexpected
publicity I ever experienced," said Annie Oakley in later years as she jotted down notes of her
memories. "The papers that were against his
courting expedition were pink with sarcastic accounts of this dashing cavalier who was outdone

at his own game by a little girl from America, of this Lochinvar who was no match for short dresses and whose warlike career faded before the onset of the American kindergarten. Whether all this had anything to do with what followed, I of course can only guess. But about that time the engagement was broken off and the opposition papers announced that 'Annie Oakley of the magic gun' had won two matches at once from the Grand Duke—the shooting trophy and the hand of the Princess, for the glory of her sex and the whole world of princesses from the Isle of Man to America."

As for the Prince of Wales, the loss of that match by the Grand Duke of Russia apparently caused but little disfavor. Certainly he showed none toward the Wild West, nor toward Miss Oakley. In fact, the Prince, popular idol of England that he was, sportsman and outdoor enthusiast, formed the greatest ally which the Buffalo Bill show possessed. There came the time when he would "drop around" unexpectedly and without his suite, drawn by the magnet of his friendship for Cody, for Miss Oakley and the entire show, for that matter. He knew the cowboys, he visited the stables and learned about bucking bronchos from the men who rode them, he talked to the Indians, with a special prefer-

ence for Red Shirt, and in an unofficial way became a sort of royal patron for the entire exhibition. As for Cody, he and the Prince of Wales
became excellent companions; Sandringham
Castle became a fairly familiar sight to a man
who once, as he expressed it, "would have been
tickled pink if the Mayor of Leavenworth, Kan.,
had deigned to shake hands with him." There
even came the time when Buffalo Bill further
cemented the bonds between England and
America by teaching His Royal Highness that
most American game—draw poker, later leading to complications for the Prince.

As for Annie Oakley, she received as much
favor. For her the Prince opened the gates of
Wimbleton, of the London Gun Club and other
sporting clubs where the average member was
of the nobility, and visiting princes were not at
all unusual. There she was given the opportunity for her first shot at the speedy "blue
rocks," wild pigeons netted on the day of a shoot
and released that afternoon that captivity might
not interfere with their speed, which was little
less than that of lightning. Her first shots at
these birds resulted in failure; her American
gun, heavily studded with gold and bearing her
image engraved upon it, was very pretty and
easy to handle. But it wasn't swift enough for

those blue rocks. Whereupon, the best gun-maker of England turned to for her, soon to present her with a pair of five pound twenty-gauge guns which she liked for this work far better than a heavier bore and with which she soon began to make surprising totals. Then it was that the Prince of Wales added to her popularity by the presentation of a medal, accompanied by the statement:

"I know no one more deserving of it."

That was the final wedge. The doors of England's society opened for her. The offerings of flowers changed to articles more intrinsic: books, dainty handkerchiefs, hand-made lace, gloves, fans and other trinkets of esteem; there even came the time when the Prince and Princess of Wales exchanged autographed photographs with a girl who once had hunted the fields and dales of Darke County, Ohio, that she might raise the money to pay off the mortgage on a poverty stricken farm.

Annie Oakley had become a sought after person. Unlike other members of the Wild West company who could but speak the vernacular, Annie Oakley possessed the poise and the education, gleaned from those years of hard study and school which had extended for years after her marriage, to adapt herself to these new surroundings in a manner which relieved the usual embarrassment which oft-times accompanies the entertainment of one lifted from the usual sphere. As for Annie Oakley's "mistake" upon her first presentation to royalty, it is this writer's opinion that she could have done differently if she chose and that her version of it was the correct one. Annie Oakley was of a type unusual to her generation. In reality a deeply religious woman, she had done that thing which, in those days, was supposed to condemn a girl to the nethermost depths of Hades, that of marrying an actor. Then, to make matters worse, she had herself become an actress. To increase the depths of her disgrace, she had joined a circus and following this had gone to the bottom of the pit by becoming the only white woman with a traveling exhibition of cowboys and other exponents of the wild and woolly west. She had done this with her eyes open, knowing the supposed consequences from a standpoint of her social status. Yet she had possessed the courage to do it, content in her own mind that her own conscience was the thing to which answers must be made after all, and if that remain clear, what else mattered? It was undoubtedly this viewpoint which caused her to shatter tradition and reach for the hand of a Princess instead of a

Prince. For in the society accounts of staid English papers, the comment columns and the spaces allotted the lampoonists who thrived in those days, there was no further evidence of a *faux pas*.

Indeed, there were plenty of opportunities, had Annie Oakley been of the uninitiated. Her life now had become almost a constant round, once her activities of the arena were over, of shooting events at the gun clubs and social affairs, a strange intermingling which London, however, seemed to enjoy thoroughly. She found herself being copied; her name had become synonymous with outdoor sportsmanship for women. Modistes attended the performances of the Buffalo Bill Wild West that they might make notes on the riding habits which she had devised—with no thought of anything save convenience and the trimness of their appearance during a performance—that society of London might have sensible riding garments like hers. Then money began its flood toward her, in amounts which she never had even visioned. The titled of London's femininity had decided that above all things, it must learn to shoot.

Annie Oakley made her price, of five dollars a pupil per day, and a class was speedily organized, the shooting grounds being that of Miss

ANNIE OAKLEY

Oakley's gunmaker which he proffered for the lessons. That caused more interest; soon a fete upon a private estate of a member of London society was not really a success without the appearance of Annie Oakley for a private exhibition of her skill as a markswoman. A fee was never mentioned; but it arrived inevitably the next day, the usual sum being $250. Annie Oakley soon found herself earning far more than a thousand dollars a week, a tremendous sum if one consider that this was forty years ago, all for doing the things she had learned while bagging quail that a roof might remain above the heads of the numerous and thoroughly unfortunate family of Jake Mozee.

To use a popular slang term, the king business was exceptionally good in the year 1887, perhaps better than it has been at any time since. It was Queen Victoria's Jubilee year, and London was the mecca of the world's royalty. With the intense interest of the Prince and Princess of Wales and other lesser lights in the Buffalo Bill show, it was inevitable that the Queen should finally become interested. However, since the death of Prince Albert, her husband, some thirty years before, Victoria had been somewhat loath to make public appearances; that she would attend a performance of the Wild West did not even enter the minds of Londoners. It was therefore with the air of looking upon a Yankee hoax that London awakened one morning to the announcement that Queen Victoria had commanded a private performance of the Wild West for five o'clock that afternoon. And if London was surprised, the outfit of the Honorable William Frederick Cody was frenzied. A day of wild preparation that, when Buffalo Bill's Wild West erected a dais and a special box, draped in crimson velvet, the performers scrambled for their best costumes, and the assemblage of vaqueros, buckin' hoss riders, shooters, buffalo killers and other exponents of the wild and woolly west made ready for the cramming of a whole performance into an hour —for Queen Victoria had stated that she could remain no longer.

Five o'clock arrived and with it the stolid, portly little woman who gave to the world the term Victorian, accompanied by the inevitable cortege of princes and princesses. Alone, phlegmatic, she sat in her box, the rest of the entourage draped about the arena in spaces prepared for them, a serious, quiet little woman, waiting to be surprised. For an hour, a frenzied, excitement-heightened gathering of show people moved before her, followed by the inevitable presentations. Among them:

"She sat in the Queen's box alone, while her suite encircled her in other boxes—" this from the notes of Annie Oakley— "She acknowledged my bow, and after my shooting she half arose from her chair, giving a queer little nod of her head and an incoming wave of her hand which indicated she wished to hold an audience with me. I stopped near, and she asked where and when I was born; at what age I took to shooting, and several other questions, and finally finished by saying 'You are a very, very clever little girl.'

"To be called clever by Queen Victoria meant that she had paid you her highest compliment, and with an 'I thank you, your Majesty,' I bowed myself out."

Evidently Queen Victoria liked her first, hurried visit to the wild west. Within a short time, London had another enthralling bit of gossip. Queen Victoria was going back, and this time with an entourage which resembled the attendance of a coronation, and for a special performance in which she would not miss an item of the program.

This time, the performance was for eleven o'clock in the morning, and the gathering of personages comprised the King of Denmark, the

A group from Buffalo Bill's Wild West Show, London, 1887. Leaning on his elbow, Pawnee Bill, who later staged a rival show.

King and Queen of Belgium, the King of Saxony, the King of Greece, the Crown Prince of Austria, the Prince and Princess of Saxe-Meiningen, the Crown Prince and Princess of Germany, with their eldest son, who later was to play such an important part in the history of the world, the Crown Prince of Sweden and Norway, the Princess Victoria of Prussia, the Duke of Sparta, the man vanquished by Annie Oakley: Grand Duke Michael of Russia, Prince George of Greece, Prince Louis of Baden and the Prince and Princess of Wales, to say nothing of the usual host of lords and ladies.

It was an interesting entertainment for the Queen, if the accounts are to be believed. It was more interesting however, for the Prince of Wales. In later years Buffalo Bill was wont to talk of that special performance and the fact that before it was over the Prince of Wales, together with four of the royal visitors from other lands, made a request to ride in the Old Deadwood Stagecoach. Then it was that Colonel Cody's poker lessons came into play.

"Colonel," Cody was wont to quote the Prince of Wales, "you never held four kings like this before."

"I've held four kings," was Buffalo Bill's reply, "But four kings and the Prince of Wales makes a royal flush and that is unprecedented."

The hair trigger laugh which was a characteristic of the Prince broke forth, bringing curiosity on the part of the other four-fifths of the hand. After that it ceased to be a joke—one does not find it so easy to explain in several languages a bit of American slang, drawn from an American card game.

It has been stated that in the personnel of that thoroughly royal visit were the Crown Prince of Germany and an eldest son. One thing seemed to interest them more than all else; it was the shooting of Annie Oakley. Before the visit had ended, an arrangement had been made whereby the Ohio crackshot would make a special visit to Germany following the engagement of the Buffalo Bill show in England, and there give a private exhibition upon the Charlottenburg racetrack at Berlin.

In Annie Oakley's notes there are some evidences that she was far too busy in giving her performance to make many observations concerning the royal personages who watched her. Little traits of character that one will notice in the distinguished persons one meets, anecdotes, unusual occurrences; these are, to a certain extent, absent. But it was not because the young woman was lacking in discernment. Before this writer is an old clipping—from the New York World of Sunday, January 8, 1888. A reporter had interviewed Annie Oakley upon her return to America.

"How did Prince Bismark impress you?" the interview runs.

"He looks like a great, shaggy mastiff. He complimented me briefly in English upon my shooting, but you ought to have heard Prince William, the young man who will succeed the Kaiser should the Crown Prince die. His eyes fairly danced with delight at my shooting, and he examined my rifle as a child would a new toy. One of his hands is crippled at the wrist, the hand turning inwards and being stiffened in that position. Yet you should have seen him examine that gun. I am sure he would be glad to go to war!"

More than a quarter of a century passed. But at last Annie Oakley's prediction came true.

Chapter Eleven

WHEN at last the years had gone and Wilhelm Hohenzollern had brought war to the world, Annie Oakley jotted down her memories of that visit, and the causes which had led her to believe that sooner or later, this man of the crippled arm would bring havoc to the universe.

The end of the London season saw a disagreement between Annie Oakley and the management of the Buffalo Bill Wild West, the only rift, in fact, which arose during the seventeen years of their association. The forces of jealousy had been at work—professional antagonism can as easily exist beneath the canvas of a tented organization as it can upon the stage—and Annie Oakley had become too popular for other members of the wild west, some of whom would like themselves to appear as the premiere feminine crackshot. There had been disagreements, arguments—at last the break became apparently unmendable. At the end of the season, after a tour of the provinces, the Buffalo Bill Wild West sailed homeward. But Frank Butler and his wife remained in Europe.

190.

ANNIE OAKLEY

For a time they contented themselves with private exhibitions and the winning of shooting matches, finally hieing themselves to Monte Carlo where huge stakes dangled and where a golden harvest seemed to await them, the purses there ranging as high as ten dollars to a bird. But the gentlemen who chose to dot the Mediterranean with the remains of fast flying pigeons, cast forth in the very shadow of the Casino, also had a great desire to take no risks with their money. Both Butler and his wife were barred on the grounds that they were professionals, and after a period of rest along the Riviera, the two turned to Berlin for the previously arranged exhibition. Miss Oakley's memories tell the rest:

"It so happened that the Emperor and the Crown Prince were both ill, so it fell to young William to conduct the affair. Never in all my life have I seen so many soldiers. I saw nothing else. The program was arranged at the Union Club in Berlin. When we had submitted a program for approval, William added the shooting of live pigeons to the events. But when· we reached the capital, we discovered that it was strictly against the law to shoot pigeons in the city. So Frank went up to the club to see about it.

"The club was inhabited exclusively by majors

and captains, field marshals and conquerors, all
in full panoply of war and bristling with side
arms and crosses. Frank ventured to explain to
the secretary that we were plain American folk
who in spite of legends to the contrary, were
prone to obey the law, and that having discovered the statute against pigeon shooting, we
would like to omit that detail from the performance.

"His answer was to push a button which summoned an orderly, and who presently appeared
with no less a person than the man who was later
to be Kaiser Wilhelm of the World War. The
situation was explained and as quickly solved.
The bell went into commission again, this time
summoning an orderly of still more imposing
aspect, His Majesty spoke:

" 'Next Sunday, Annie Oakley will give an
exhibition at Charlottenburg. You will see that
the chief of police and none other of the police
are admitted while it is going on!'

"This was his manner of doing things while
he was still the grandson of the reigning monarch. Fancy what he became after the government fell into his hands. I remember that at
the time I started to say 'war mad!' to my husband. His use of the same words interrupted
me, and our next trip to Germany, after Wil-

helm had actually become emperor proved our belief beyond any doubt."

Back in America, following an order to cancel an engagement in Paris because of threatened illness, Annie Oakley announced that she would not again appear with the Buffalo Bill show. For a time, trap shooting events occupied her entire attention, during which she won the deciding match of the event begun with the English champion at the time her hand was injured by the premature springing of a trap. Then, quite innocently she took part in one of those queer little tricks of Fate by which the mills of the gods gain credit for the fineness of their grist.

Contracts had been made for a later date, to appear in vaudeville and also in a play, in which Annie Oakley was to become a "dramatic star." A space of time intervened, and an offer had come from a newly forming Wild West company to fill in that time as one of its stars. The contract was accepted, for a larger amount of money than Annie Oakley had yet drawn, and shortly before the time for the beginning of rehearsals, Mrs. Butler and her husband journeyed from New York to the exposition grounds to look over their new home in the show world.

It was a disappointing visit. A group of In-

ANNIE OAKLEY

dians were camped on the rehearsal grounds, together with a large number of horses and a small group of men who called themselves cowboys. But as one led forth a horse to attempt an exhibition of riding, Butler shook his head.

"It's no go, Missy," he said. "We can't afford to be connected with a failure."

There was every indication that the show would be nothing but that. It was being promoted by a ferry boat company and a Philadelphia multi-millionaire, who, knowing nothing of the wild west business themselves, had trusted to persons who, according to Annie Oakley's description, wore imitation Stetson hats, and were as real in their knowledge of the west as they were in their headgear. The cowboys could not ride, there was no management, there was nothing in fact to indicate that the show would go farther than its first performance. Hastily the pair journeyed to Philadelphia in an effort to break the contract. It was useless; the agreement had been made and they must live up to it.

In the meanwhile, another man was having his troubles. Back in the opening days of the Buffalo Bill show, he had been the one to obtain Pawnee Indians for it, owing to the fact that he was an honorary member of the tribe and a

194.

teacher of the Pawnees. His name was Lillie, Gordon W. Lillie, his nickname that of Pawnee Bill. A year or so with the wild west show had given him ambitions to own an organization of his own.

Therefore he had started, with much enthusiasm and little else, fighting his way along from town to town, often but one jump ahead of the sheriff, but struggling nevertheless. And as he struggled, he realized that a great and powerful foe blocked his way—the foe who once had been his friend. But friendships in the show world last only as long as there is not a clash of canvas. With Pawnee Bill's entrance into the wild west amusement business, there naturally had come the antagonism of the swift-growing Buffalo Bill organization; the old rule was that a show must crush or be crushed. Pawnee Bill now was experiencing the effects of the steam roller.

Fresh from its European triumphs and with a bigger show than it ever had known before, the Buffalo Bill Wild West now was throttling everything in its path. It was all-powerful; the millions were rolling in, and there must be no impediment to the steady flow of wealth. Consequently, as it happens even now in the outdoor amusement world, the agents of the Buffalo Bill show worked unceasingly that the Pawnee Bill

195.

aggregation might suffer as much as possible. Time after time, Major Lillie booked his struggling aggregation into a town only to find that the billposters of the all-powerful Buffalo Bill exhibition had covered his paper—that is, pasted advertisements of the Buffalo Bill Wild West over those of the Pawnee Bill outfit—and announced a show on the same date, to which the patrons would flood, leaving Pawnee Bill to gaze at empty seats where otherwise there might have been throngs. Now the battle was ending, and as Frank Butler boarded a ferry with one of the backers of the newly forming wild west, his eye caught a headline of a proffered paper in the hands of a newsboy. It stated:

"Pawnee Bill Show Stranded in Pittsburgh."

Hastily he read the article which announced the details of an attachment for several thousand dollars which had formed the final blow against the little aggregation. The news had been given to the papers, quite strangely, by Major John M. Burke, press agent for Buffalo Bill. Butler turned hurriedly to the wild west impresario.

"Here's your chance!" he exclaimed. "I can see through this thing—the Buffalo Bill outfit has engineered this in some way. It's an old trick, to work up an attachment to get rid of an opposition amusement. The thing for you to do is to jump on a train, go out there to Pittsburgh, free this company of its debt, load it on a special train and bring it here. Then you'll have a name to work with, an organization to build on and something to make a show with instead of that imitation outfit you've got now."

The argument was won. The magnate hurried to Pittsburgh, there to rescue a very lugubrious Pawnee Bill and his entire outfit and bring them to Staten Island. Only a week remained to make ready for the opening, and while the rehearsals were held, there thundered from the billboards, from roadway signs, from the walls of barns and every other conceivable place, the fighting announcement of the Buffalo Bill aggregation, so well known to those who have endured the thrills of a circus warfare:

"WAIT FOR THE BIG SHOW!
BUFFALO BILL IS COMING."

The date was exactly four weeks after that of the new aggregation which then was rehearsing —against odds. Everything was in a tangle— two sets of Indians, two sets of bucking horses, two sets of everything, but someway between

197.

ANNIE OAKLEY

Annie Oakley, Frank Butler and Pawnee Bill
they managed to straighten it out. Upon one
person alone did the success or the failure of that
show rest. That was Annie Oakley.

The old fighting instinct was strong within the
girl who had gained much of experience by
fighting, in one way or another, for the greater
part of her existence. Once the news of her contract with the other management had been announced, there had come a call to what was then
little less than a throne—the office of Nate Salsbury.

"Don't you take that contract!" she was urged.

"But I've already signed."

"Then break it. Or we'll fight you."

Just what it was that Annie Oakley said following that statement she never revealed. But
when she was through, Nate Salsbury smiled,
and rose with the announcement:

"No, Annie. You're right. No matter what
happens, we won't fight you!"

That was said in the personal sense. No
promise was made for the show itself and Annie
Oakley, now that she had been threatened, was
cast for the battlefield. She was the new show's
star performer, she the one upon whom everything depended. The show opened. Annie
Oakley performed, on horseback, on foot, at

198.

"press agent stunts;" she gave interviews, she displayed the innumerable cups and medals which had come to her as the results of her shooting prowess both in America and abroad. She had become the backbone of the whole show, the reason for its existence, the recommendation for it. And she drew the crowds. The show prospered—even the overtowering strength of the Buffalo Bill Wild West could not keep the crowds from its gates.

Now for the sequel. In the formation of that show, Major Gordon W. Lillie formed associations which lasted him through the entire life of his showmanship. Men who would come to his rescue in times of stress, who would back him for new ventures, and upon ideas which others might have denied. It was his true beginning—with the exception of the time which he spent in southern Kansas as one of the boomers of the new state of Oklahoma—his life for a quarter of a century after that was given to the wild west business. He met reverses and beat them. Steadily he climbed; the impetus given him during the time Annie Oakley was associated with the show, the possibilities of the business, sent Pawnee Bill higher and higher in the amusement world, despite every effort of rival shows to hold him down. At last there came the time

when rich, powerful, Major Gordon W. Lillie
was approached by the executor of the estate
which owned the Buffalo Bill Wild West. The
show had passed from the hands of Nate Salsbury. It had passed from the possession of Buffalo Bill himself. Now, moneyless, in debt, what
small interest he held in the show mortgaged, the
millions which had flowed into his hands gone to
the four winds, Colonel William Frederick
Cody was a beaten man. And it was Pawnee
Bill, the young showman whom he had fought,
nearly a quarter of a century before, and whom
Annie Oakley had rescued as, stranded, broke,
he looked over the wreckage of his show on the
lot at Pittsburgh, who bought the Buffalo Bill
show, threw into it the old, shrewd system of
management which it had known back in the
days of Nate Salsbury, enabled it to make money
and practically gave back to William Frederick
Cody the half interest which had been dissipated. When Annie Oakley and her husband
had saved Pawnee Bill's show, that it might be
used as a weapon of defense against the great
Buffalo Bill organization, they in reality began
the upward career of the man who someday
could call himself the true owner of the big
show which once had all but caused his downfall
as a showman.

200.

ANNIE OAKLEY

These days might be called barnstorming ones for Annie Oakley. When her short contract with the new Wild West expired, she hurried to a waiting one which called for exhibitions in vaudeville. Then, that done, she went to another, in which she learned the rather eventful life of a melodrama star.

The life of a stage character had been painted in bright colors, principally because the promoter possessed little more than a play, and saw in Annie Oakley a chance to capitalize a name which now was known throughout America. But Miss Oakley didn't know that at the time; little details like that are sometimes carefully concealed. The contract had been made, in fact, before she gained the slightest inkling of it, and the play was in rehearsal.

It should have been worth seeing, that play. The name of it, lest there be some belief that it had to do with lavender and old lace, was the he-man title of "Deadwood Dick." There were "Injuns," and prospectors, and bad men galore, there was a sweet, innocent, starry-eyed chee-ild, who, out upon the broad prairee, knelt before the footlights and said his prayers—just before the Indians attacked—in a manner which the management guaranteed to bring tears to an iron hitching post. There was the inevitable man gone wrong through drink, a fine, stalwart, rough-diamond of a fellow, who, had it not been for the Demon Rum might have made his mark in the world. As it was, about the only marks he could make were by becoming crocked to the gunwales and denting the ground by doing wing-dings on his head. There was the motherly pioneer's wife, the sturdy, silent, bearded man coming into the west to make his fortune, and then there was Annie Oakley. One review of the play read:

"Regarding the play, the shooting of Annie Oakley was very good."

As for Miss Oakley's comment, it was crisp; going but little farther than to still wonder, years afterward, why the audiences had refrained from throwing vegetables.

After a time, the suspicion became more than well confirmed that this was an outlandish attempt to make money upon a name, a gambling venture taken upon a shoestring. Miss Oakley so shaped her affairs that it was possible for her to leave, and this she did. The show ran a few weeks, became faulty in the payment of salaries and suddenly collapsed overnight. It was about this time that Nate Salsbury and Buffalo Bill,

202.

planning for the future, remarked to Annie Oakley that perhaps their differences were not too great for eradication after all. Miss Oakley held the same opinion—the Buffalo Bill Wild West was home to her. There were meetings, a consideration of the causes which had led her to leave the show after its London engagement, and then a welcomed announcement went forth. It was that the Buffalo Bill show was returning to Europe, there to begin its tour by forming one of the main attractions at the Paris Exhibition of 1889. Again Miss Annie Oakley would be its shooting star.

Luck plays its part in more than one success— especially in the amusement field. Annie Oakley was taken back to the fold simply because friendship and worth demanded it; Nate Salsbury and Buffalo Bill looked upon her as little less than a daughter; her affection for the two men was as deep and the disagreement had caused pain on both sides. She was a star who drew the crowds, and they wanted her for that reason, just as Annie Oakley was glad to go back because the prestige and the background of the great wild west enhanced her act. But had these things not come to a point of settlement just at this time and had Annie Oakley not gone to Europe on the second trip of the Buffalo Bill

Wild West, there might have been a different story of that second tour, and it is highly possible that the Buffalo Bill show at Paris would have been a failure.

The place of exhibition was the Parc de Neuilly, just outside the Ternes gates of the Paris fortifications. Today, one would reach it merely by proceeding along the Avenue de la Grande Armee from the Place de l'Etoile at the end of the Champs Elysees, a scant ten minutes in a careening taxicab from that most American gathering place in the center of Paris, the Cafe de la Paix. A most convenient showgrounds; this and the London representation of the show, the favors of royalty, the command performance before Queen Victoria, the gathering of practically every ruler and potentate during the Jubilee year, had caused considerable comment on Buffalo Bill's show in Paris. The result was that the opening day found the President of the Republic, his wife, artists like Meissonier, Detaille, and others accompanied by twenty thousand French men and women crammed in the place of exhibition with the typically Missourianese attitude of desiring to be shown.

The grand entree of the show arrived, without as much as a ripple of applause from the audience. The first acts went on, and still the tremendous mass of twenty thousand persons sat graven. Buffalo Bill began to pull at his goatee, a sure evidence of nervousness, while Nate Salsbury adopted a short, jerky pacing step at the rear entrance, with quick glances toward the audience, as though any instant might change its demeanor. But Paris, such of it at least, that was crowded into the Buffalo Bill ampitheater, gave no evidence whatever of changing in any particular. A cowboy, fresh from having fought a sunfishing outlaw horse over most of the arena, slipped from the arms of his pick-up man, dropped to the ground, made his grandiloquent bow and received—silence.

"Shore is cold here in Paris, ain't it?" he asked as he reached the exit. "Must be full ten inches o' frost on thet audience."

As the show progressed, it became even more frosty. Colonel Cody began to emit suppressed bellows of concern, somewhat like the rumblings of Vesuvius, heard at a distance. Nate Salsbury turned hurriedly and summoned an interpreter.

"Get up into the grandstand," he commanded, "and see what the trouble is. Ask some of those people—if they're not deaf and dumb—why they don't like the show."

Then as the interpreter moved away, he switched the program slightly, that he might send the old Deadwood Stagecoach careening about the arena, with the red fire glaring and the Sioux and Kiowas pursuing it in the approved style. This brought no more enthusiasm than the rest of the entertainment, and Salsbury hurried forward anxiously at the sight of the interpreter.

"What is it?" he asked.

"Well," said the interpreter. "These people, they do not understand what it is about. They object to all this pretending."

"Pretending?" asked Cody and Salsbury in one breath. "What pretending?"

"The bucking horses, for instance. They feel that it is just a show, because they say that if horses were that mean, why should anybody try to ride them?"

"They call that pretendin'?" asked Cody. "Dog my cats, that last cowpuncher came pretty near being killed."

"That is exactly the case," said the interpreter. "I told that to the people with whom I talked. And they asked me: *'Voila!* Why should he want to kill himself?'"

"But the Indians," interjected Salsbury. "You'd think that they'd get up some interest in

206.

the Indians. Don't they know that these are actual chiefs and braves who fought against the United States Army for the possession of the West? Don't they—?"

"They don't," the interpreter answered. "You see, I brought up that point also, and they answered me by saying *'Mon Dieu! Do you expect us to believe that they would actually turn such fierce savages loose to kill everybody in sight if they cared to?'* It is an imitation, they say."

William Frederick Cody allowed his tongue to sag from the corner of his lips and wagged his head in solemn despair; the problem had gone beyond him. Nate Salsbury frowned, stared about him, then suddenly started forward at the sight of Annie Oakley, just coming forward to make her entrance, followed by her attendant with the guns.

"Missy!" he commanded, "you've got to do something! You're the last card. These Frenchmen out here can't tell a Comanche from a drug store, or a horse from a walking beam. They think everything in the show is just an imitation. Get out there and prove that it isn't."

It was about the most difficult assignment which Annie Oakley ever had received. But there was nothing to do except to make an honest attempt to carry out the commands. Since the audience was giving but scant courtesy to any performer, Annie Oakley adopted the same attitude toward the audience and walked into the great, bare arena with a perceptible chip on her shoulder. She acknowledged the audience, and that was all—a scant bob of the head, as though she were speaking to a bare acquaintance, then she turned with a command to her assistants and object holders. The guns came forward; Annie Oakley began to shoot with as little concern for those who watched as though she were conducting a rehearsal.

One by one the rifle tricks were gone through, and Annie Oakley heard the audience, with a perceptible rustle, settle as with a concentration of interest. Before this, there had been a constant current of conversation, the rustle of newspapers, the calling of gamins one to another. Now however, that had ceased, and Miss Oakley, realizing that the audience at last had found something it could understand, the art of shooting, became more friendly.

Finally, at a difficult pistol shot, there was a slight ripple of applause. Annie Oakley acknowledged it; realizing that her contest not yet was won; so far she had done things which had been seen upon the stage and which could be faked by a clever performer. But when she came to her shotgun work, there was no such possibility. With that came the climax.

The "Little Missy" lifted a double barrelled shotgun and commanded that two glass balls be thrown into the air at once. There was a double report, and the objects shattered, while the first real applause of the premiere performance broke forth from the packed stands. Out in the entrance, Nate Salsbury turned to his worried partner.

"By God, Bill!" he exclaimed, "she's saved the show."

"Dog my cats if she ain't," answered Buffalo Bill, only to be interrupted by another burst of applause. Four balls had gone into the air, working like lightning with two guns, Annie Oakley had shattered them all.

Gun work was something that this French audience knew. Practically every man in the audience had served his time in the standing army; many sportsmen were there, officers, members of the Foreign Legion. Shooting and its difficulties were well known affairs. But Annie hadn't ceased. She tried the trick of laying down her gun, jumping over a table, springing two birds from a trap and landing them both before they struck the ground. She did her trick of turning around while the objects flew through the air, and getting them before she stopped whirling. Everything she ever had done to amaze an audience she did now, finally turning to a trick which she did not often perform in the ring, that of using three shotguns to demolish six glass balls thrown into the air.

Like the reports of a machine gun came the banging of those shotguns. One after another the missiles broke, so quickly that it was almost impossible to follow the destruction with the eye. Then bowing, she retired, while hats waved, arms went into the air, men and women rose from their seats and even the President stood to bow to her. It was as though this little woman, by demonstrating feats deemed impossible by the audience had given a guarantee of the reality of the entire show. If this wonderful shooting could be real, then the Indians were real, and the stagecoach and the riders and the wild horses and everything else in keeping. Annie Oakley strove to retire. Impossible. The show had been stopped by cries of "Bravo" and "Vive l'Annie Oakley."! Salsbury pushed her to the entrance.

"Go back and give 'em some more!" he commanded and the laughing Annie Oakley obeyed, only to be called back again and again and again to a repetition of her act for the fifth time before the audience subsided. After that, there was no doubt of the success of the Buffalo Bill show in Paris. The name of it was on the tongue of everyone, with the principal emphasis however, upon an adjunct, that of the "Little Missy."

Time worn and weather beaten, there is in the collection left by Miss Oakley, one of the tickets used to gain admission to the Buffalo Bill Wild West Show during that engagement. Like all French billets, it bears the inevitable advertisements of "aperitifs," confidential detectives, cafés, mineral waters and what-not. But in one particular, it is different from most admission cards. For it bears a double announcement which reads, on one side:

Un Billet
Premiere Classe

Buffalo Bill Wild West.

While on the other is a statement, which, in English, would read:

"This ticket enables the bearer to see the great markswoman, Annie Oakley."

Chapter Twelve

THE Paris engagement became a small counterpart of the one in England. In fact, if possible, Miss Oakley received a greater amount of encomiums than had been her lot at Earl's Court. Paris idolized her. The shooting clubs followed her about with invitations to become an honorary member—clubs, incidentally, which included the pick of the royalty of Europe. Sadri Carnot was then President of France, Miss Oakley met him first in the arena, then at the President's palace. Finally there came the time, on parting, when the President said:

"When you feel like changing your nationality and profession, there is a commission awaiting you in the French army."

Which, indeed, was a more alluring prospect than another position offered Miss Oakley during her Paris engagement, or rather, offered Buffalo Bill for her. Potentates of distant lands were not unusual at the Wild West Exhibition. The Shah of Persia was one of the visitors, the Sultan of Turkey, and a third was Dina Salifour, King of Senegal, who watched the exhibition of Miss Oakley with more than ordinary interest. Finally, he turned and talked volubly to his advisors and, following the performance, the king sought Buffalo Bill.

"How much do you want for her?" he asked, after a long dilation upon the wonders of the "Little Missy." Buffalo Bill pulled at his goatee.

"Want for her?" he asked in nonplussed manner, "how do you mean?"

"To sell her. I wish to take her back with me. In my country," he added naively, "my people are not safe in many of the small villages. There are man-eating tigers in many districts, and even one of these animals can cause much damage. But with a person of such wonderful skill as she, it would be easy to organize parties with her as the chief huntress; the danger would be soon past. Would you consider a hundred thousand francs sufficient?"

The eyes of Buffalo Bill glinted, but that was the only indication of humor. He summoned an orderly.

"Tell Miss Oakley to come here," he commanded and the crackshot obeyed. "Missy," said Colonel Cody, "I've got an awful good offer for you here." He then introduced the King of Senegal. "His Majesty would like to buy you for a hundred thousand francs to go down to his country and shoot man-eating tigers."

The fun of baiting a king, even a naive one, did not arise every day.

"But am I for sale, Colonel?" Miss Oakley asked seriously.

"Come to think of it, I guess you ain't," the buffalo killer answered. It was a signal to the King of Senegal to exert his best oratory. He raised his price, and then, as a finale, begged Buffalo Bill to release his slave.

"Slave?" asked Cody. "She isn't any slave. She's the one to say whether she wants to go down there or not. I haven't anything to do with it outside of her contract."

The King seemed worried.

"Not a slave?" he asked.

"Nope, not a slave."

It was time for apologies and the King of Senegal made them. Following this, he tried his argument upon Miss Oakley herself. And when that failed:

"When I told him I did not wish to go," say Miss Oakley's notes, "he went down on one knee with a sweeping grace that would have done credit to ye knights of old England, and lifting my hand, raised my fingertips to his lips. He departed with the air of a soldier." The woman

214.

who as a girl had shot off the mortgage on a backwoods home in Darke County, Ohio, went, in quite manner of fact fashion, back to her tent, her medals, her souvenirs, and her visitors. Kings, queens and other forms of royalty had become more of a staple article than when she gave her first performance before the Prince of Wales.

The stay in Paris lasted until November. Then came Marseilles, with a small replica of the Paris engagement, Lyons and, after that, one of the grimmest experiences that ever befell an exhibition in a foreign land. It was in Spain, at Barcelona.

Evidently the fictioneers and songsters who had thrilled over the town had denuded it of its romantic gestures by the time the Buffalo Bill show arrived. The town was dirty, poverty stricken; the Buffalo Bill show pitched its tents amidst a perfect congress of beggars who screamed and fought and struggled like so many hyenas for every scrap thrown from the mess tents. A survey of the town, of the shops and of the populace caused a conference, at which it was decided that, should the regular admission prices be charged, it was more than probable that no one would attend. Therefore the scale was cut, to perhaps the lowest admission at which the Buffalo Bill Wild West ever exhibited. Then the gates of the show opened.

There seemed some hope of a growing attendance to judge from the first crowd, which scattered the ampitheater. But when the show was half over, a hurrying treasurer sought Nate Salsbury with exciting news. Of the six hundred dollars which had been taken in, more than three hundred of it was counterfeit!

"Guess we'd better make a complaint to the chief of police about it," was the verdict after the story was told. This was accordingly done, with but scant satisfaction. The chief of police was indeed sorry. But the Buffalo Bill show was not the only one to suffer from spurious coin. Only that day, a storekeeper had been arrested on the charge of counterfeiting the government's money, and had made the surprising plea that while it was true that he had been coining his own cash, it was so much better than the money which the government was putting forth that he felt that he had committed no crime. More, the judge had congratulated him upon his artistry— and allowed him to go free!

Perhaps no American aggregation of show people ever found itself in stranger circumstances. As Annie Oakley told it years later:

"After this information had been received,

216.

the boys of the show figured it out that since counterfeiting seemed to be a sort of municipal pastime, the game should have two sides to it. They therefore sauntered into the midway, which might have been Main Street, determined to return some of the tinware which had been accumulated by the show, in return for coffee, bran and other necessities. It was impossible. The passing of counterfeit money was an art, it seemed, chiefly enjoyed by Barcelonians, and others who did not possess the education in deception necessary to the finer points of the game were badly handicapped.

"Every shopkeeper was armed and prepared for just such an emergency—or rather, for just such a certainty. In fact, it seemed, their constant occupation was a suspicious and exhaustive inquiry into the origin, nature and composition of the customer's coin. Every counter possessed a marble slab, over which the storekeeper bent to learn the desires of his customers. It was not at all hard, even though we did not know the language, to make known what we wanted, but to pay for it was an entirely different matter. The first thing, of course, was to pass over the coin, whereupon the storekeeper would gaze at it as though it had offended every ancestor of his family. Then with a furious gesture, he would throw it upon that marble slab in the first of the tests as to its genuineness.

"That first test often was enough, for the coin usually broke. Many of the spurious pieces of money were made of nothing but glass; naturally they could not withstand the first onslaught. But if they did it then went through another system of dropping and throwing, during which time it was determined whether it contained lead, tin or other base ingredients. If the coin stood all these tests, it then was passed on to the weigher who compared the inscriptions and the avoirdupois with a table of figures which he kept close at hand. Then, horror of horrors, if it passed inspection there, you got change. Pocketsfull of change, worth nothing, except to an iron foundry! One can imagine, with this elaborate system of learning whether a dollar's worth of coin was really a dollar's worth or entirely useless, what chance a show would have to keep track of the good and bad money. In fact, it meant close figuring to feed the stock and raise enough real money to buy food for the cookhouse. Nobody even dreamed of drawing a salary, until the show could get into a land where there was real money and where we could establish communications with the United States by which to receive remittances. They were not safe here; the

A quaint portrait from the family album.

best New York draft in the world might only result in bales of counterfeit money. And this with Christmas in a foreign land approaching, to say nothing of illness."

That was the worst of the winter of 1889-1890 in Spain, when the Buffalo Bill show, marooned, almost penniless, unable to move, all but faced extinction. Typhoid was rampant, and small-pox—three deaths were accredited to this disease in the workingmen's and Indian's section of the show, while influenza and typhoid ravaged every department. But the show went on, there was nothing else to do; afternoon following afternoon the performances were given, often only to gatherings of mendicants and loafers; there were even times when an admission price equivalent to ten cents American money could not draw the crowds; many did not even have that amount to spend on amusement. By this time, Barcelona had been quarantined; that was about the sole extent of the battle which Spain was waging against its onslaught of disease.

Seven more of the Indians died; the show went on. Workingmen succumbed to the dread small-pox; the gathering of Americans burned their clothing and effects, and continued their afternoon performances. Then, two days before Christmas, Frank Butler staggered into the damp room in which he and Annie Oakley lived, gaunt eyed from fatigue and illness.

"Frank's going to die," he said hollowly. He referred to Frank Richmond, the orator of the show, who had been the one to present Annie Oakley to the Prince of Wales and Queen Victoria. "I've left Johnny Baker with him. He'll call me if things get worse."

At midnight the summons came. At three o'clock the next afternoon, a weary, fever stricken contingent from the show stood in the long line before the local cemetery, awaiting their turn to enter with the body of a friend, which they desired to place in a vault until arrangements could be made to transfer it to America. So great were the casualties, so heavy the burial burden of the scourge of small-pox, typhoid and influenza, that the mourning friends waited from three o'clock in the afternoon until nine o'clock at night, before it was possible to place the body of Frank Richmond in a vault.

Frank Butler was ill now, and Annie Oakley. Yet so strong was the showman instinct, that in spite of the counterfeit money, and ragged beggars of an audience:

"Shortly after noon I tried to raise my head from my pillow, but fell back. After four or five attempts, I succeeded. A costume lay on the trunk near the bed. I reached it by grasping the trunk covering and pulling it all over near me. An hour and a half were spent in partly dressing; then I decided to try standing, but I kept hold of the bed as I did so. I careened about the room toward an open window and finally made it, but fainted as I grasped the low sill. However, I took my place in the arena that afternoon."

In spite of all, it was determined that there must be a Christmas turkey. Frank Butler and Johnny Baker, both ill, but determined, started forth in search of one. At the first shop, Baker enquired in Spanish:

"Have you a turkey?"

"Yes," came the reply, "which part will you have, a leg, a wing, or a liver?"

It was an indication of the poverty of the city; conditions had become so terrible that whole fowls were not being sold; happy indeed was he who could buy even a piece of one! The Americans made it known that they wanted a whole bird; when they at last procured it, they were forced to fight their way through a mass of more than two hundred beggars to reach their hotel. But there was turkey for that Christmas day.

Arrangements were at last made for an escape from Spain; it was little else. It was not hard

ANNIE OAKLEY

to enlist the aid of officers, and to evade the various regulations thrown about the city; on January 20, 1890, a shattered wild west company set sail from Barcelona upon a miserable tub of a boat so badly ballasted that the pilot at first refused to take her outside the harbor. But this was a matter of taking one risk that a greater one might be avoided; the company persisted in its desire to leave, and with one terrific storm rolling before it and another following, the overburdened craft finally made its way to Naples and to a new beginning for the Wild West. Even the alley-like, greasy, garbage strewn streets of Naples, the thousands of beggars, the filth, were heavenly compared with Barcelona.

Italy formed a lucrative territory for the Buffalo Bill Wild West; soon the losses of Barcelona had been recouped by the proceeds of the engagements in Naples, in Rome, in artistic Florence, Pisa, Milan and Verona, where performances were given in the ancient stone arena which had existed for centuries. After that, the border was crossed into Bavaria and Annie Oakley learned how it felt to save the life of a king.

Rather a Prince Regent, for Luitpold of Bavaria ruled in the stead of the mad King Otto, confined for years in his palace of Furstenried, guarded by picked soldiers and surrounded by

ANNIE OAKLEY

a wall so high that the public could not even gain a glimpse of the grounds. One morning, shortly after the opening at Munich, the Regent's messenger arrived at the showgrounds, enquired for Fraulein Oakley, and delivered the message:

"If convenient, His Majesty requests the honor of an audience with Fraulein Oakley at 10:30 this morning."

Naturally, the request was granted. At 10:30 o'clock, a carriage drove into the showgrounds. There was no ostentation, no retinue, no suite; Prince Luitpold had gained his hold upon the Bavarian people shortly after the deposing of the mad monarch by the announcement that he would accept no extra emoluments from the Bavarian treasury for his new position, and that he was only a ruler in lieu of one who was incapacitated to rule for himself. Only his coachman and footman accompanied him to the Wild West grounds, and he approached the tent of Annie Oakley for a chat, while cowpunchers lolled in the background, Indians grunted at the sight of democratic royalty, performers passed to and fro to their rehearsals and the Wild West proceeded without much more excitement than would be caused by the visit of the mayor of an American city. To judge from Annie Oakley's

223.

notes, one becomes accustomed quite easily to royalty. Or did, thirty-five years ago, when there was more of it than exists now.

The Prince Regent was interested in shooting. He examined the guns which Annie Oakley used in the ring, he looked at her medals and trophies, won in various parts of the world during competitive meets at shooting clubs. Then, after the usual questions which are asked of an unusual person, the Prince Regent came to the object of his visit.

"I would like very much," he said, "to have a souvenir of your work. Do you suppose that if I should throw a coin into the air, you could hit it with a pistol?"

Annie Oakley, said in good, Ohio American, that she guessed she could. Together they passed along the line of horse-tents, dressing tents where cowgirls were hanging out their washing, Indian tepees, and into the arena. At one side, several cowboys were attempting to tame the spirits of a newly imported bucking horse, which answered—when it chose—to the endearing term of Dynamite. Two of them, with teeth bared, chewed amiably on the outlaw's ears; a device for cooling the spirits of equine outlaws, now barred in rodeos by an edict of the Humane Society. Another held a gunnysack tightly over the animal's eyes, while a fourth went gingerly about the business of easing a saddle upon the quivering back, and tightening the cinch. All this while the Prince Regent tossed the coin into the air, Annie Oakley plugged it with a shot from the revolver, and the ruler of Bavaria pocketed the souvenir with many thanks. Just then Annie Oakley glanced toward the spraddled Dynamite, bunching its muscles as a cowboy swung to the saddle.

"We're in danger here!" she said. The Prince Regent followed her glance and shrugged his shoulders. Bucking horses were new to him; like the Parisians, he thought that they were "just trained to act that way."

"I don't believe he will hurt us," said the Prince Regent, and an instant later changed his mind. Before either the Prince or Miss Oakley could retreat, Dynamite, the bit between his teeth and his head down, carrying his rider helpless and rolling upon his back, had streaked across the arena and was within a few plunging feet of the monarch. A lightning move and Miss Oakley leaped, lunging with all her strength against Luitpold and throwing him from his feet and a short distance to one side. Dynamite came down from a bucking leap, four feet bunched, where the monarch had been only an instant before, while Annie Oakley, still jerking and tugging at the ruler, pulled him to safety, as the wild horse brushed his shoulder and went bucking across the arena.

"You were right," laughed the Prince as hurrying flunkeys rushed forward to brush him off, "there was danger, wasn't there?"

After that, the matter was apparently dismissed; Luitpold talked again of Miss Oakley's shooting and of the Wild West as he partook of a camp breakfast, and then his visit done, entered his carriage once more for his palace. But the next day, there arrived an evidence that he had not dismissed the incident. It was a token for Miss Oakley, in gratitude for having saved the life of the ruler of Bavaria, a diamond bracelet, valued heavily in the thousands, and bearing the crown and monogram of Luitpold.

Vienna followed Munich, with more royalty, and a meeting with the Emperor of Austria in his palace. Regarding that meeting, incidentally, Annie Oakley in her notes put into a few words her whole opinion of the august persons whom she had met during her exhibition days, and the attitude of mind which she held toward them. There are those, of course, who even today believe that the term "royalty" carries with it some mysterious power of an anointment

by God. That feeling was much stronger thirty
or forty years ago, before dethronements, as-
sassinations, abdications, wars and the influx of
democracy into Europe had wiped out many of
the traditions so carefully fostered by lines of
hereditary rulers. Then a duke amounted to a
great deal in the world, a prince was a sensation and a king—if one could meet a king—was
something to talk about for the rest of one's life.
Annie Oakley carried a peculiar bump of common sense. She saw in them persons not favored
by Deity as many persons actually imagined at
the time, but humans heightened by power. As
for the glamor of it:

"I really felt sorry when I looked into the
face of the Emperor of Austria. My husband
and I were being shown through the palace one
morning and the Emperor sat at a table stacked
high with mail for his perusal, but somehow he
asked that I be shown into his august presence.
He arose with a smile and greeted me with a
real handshake, but his face looked both tired
and troubled. I then and there decided that
being just plain little Annie Oakley with ten
minutes work once or twice a day, was good
enough for me, for I had, or at least I thought I
had, my freedom."

Dresden followed Vienna, with the favors of

227.

the Duchess of Holstein, and her daughter Princess Fedora, with a shoot on the King's game preserve and the usual attentions of royalty. Magdeburg, Braunschweig and Leipzig followed. Hamburg, Bremen, Cologne, Dusseldorf, Frankfort on Main, Stuttgart, then Strassburg, where the show halted for the winter. The day before closing, Frank Butler and his wife stepped into their tent to find Colonel Cody sitting there, at Miss Oakley's table. He rose abruptly and left. Then they noticed that Miss Oakley's autograph book lay open, and signed as it was by practically every ruler of Europe, bore a freshly written inscription, which to Annie Oakley meant more than all the rest. It read:

"To the loveliest and truest little woman, both in heart and aim in all the world. Sworn to by and before myself. W. F. Cody, Buffalo Bill, Strassburg, 1890."

228.

Chapter Thirteen

IT was a rather lonely company which saw the end of the season of 1890 at Strassburg. For with their farewell to the performances of the year, they were giving a farewell also to their chief. Colonel William Frederick Cody was going back to America and to what might be the battlefield.

There are those who have called Buffalo Bill an eternal showman. But Buffalo Bill was something more than that; he was an intense patriot with the showmanship instinct.

Indian affairs had not been good at home. There had been ill-treatment of the Sioux on the Pine Ridge reservation, with the accompanying objections of the various tribes to what they termed starvation. Sitting Bull had been making his demands at Washington for better treatment of his people. The "Indian Question" had arisen again, to occupy the front pages of the newspapers and accordingly to be the subject of conversation at many gatherings. Then, a mistaken zealot—who he was never has been determined—sent forth word to the various tribes that he was Christ come to earth again, and that if the various tribes would send their representatives to a meeting place at Pyramid Lake, Nevada, he would outline a plan by which all could be peace again.

How those representatives made the long journey is almost beyond comprehension. Short Bull, for instance, the representative of the Ogallala Sioux, traveled from a spot near Manderson, South Dakota, across what was then a country with but few roads and no rail transportation, making a part of the distance on horseback and part of it on foot. Other representatives accomplished the journey in the same fashion. Christ had come back to earth to aid the Indian. And the Indian, suffering and destitute, was willing to believe almost anything.

"Christ," as he existed at Pyramid Lake, Nevada, was different indeed from the Being described in the Scriptures. This Messiah was much older and possessed a son which he presented to the Indian chiefs without explanation. A demented white man with a knowledge of magic and evidently a store of electric batteries, he performed various feats for the Indians, and appeared and disappeared by the simple routine of jumping from behind a large rock and retiring in the same way. His message was that the

Indian should adopt religion, and to this end, he passed forth a queerly marked white shirt which he called the Ghost Shirt and which was to be worn at religious ceremonial dances. Then, having adopted religion, the Indian was to intermingle with the whites, marry and bring paleface husbands and wives into the tribes. If this were done, he said, the grass of the prairie once more would grow green and the buffalo would again roam the plains. Of course, he was speaking figuratively, with the meaning that if his idea were followed, prosperity would come to the Indian. But while the red man has a habit of talking in figures of speech, he also has an intense literal inclination. The representatives went back and reported what had been told them by the Messiah. What followed afterwards was a little piece of Indian politics.

This writer is one of the few white persons to whom Short Bull, blamed for the "Ghost Shirt War" ever told his story. That recital, given during a blizzard in a weaving tent on the South Dakota prairies, was one of Indian politics in which Short Bull averred that his report had been twisted into one demanding war against the whites, and in which the Ghost Shirts, instead of being merely part of a religious rite, after having been blessed by him, became bullet proof in the eye of the Sioux warriors.

War was looming when Buffalo Bill closed his show. Hurriedly he set sail for America, to take his position as Brigadier General of the state troops of Nebraska, operating under the guidance of General Miles, then in command of the Department of the Missouri. Orders had gone forth to arrest Sitting Bull. Colonel Cody started from Chicago, in an effort to reach the old Indian chieftain before the police. But he failed. Sitting Bull, he who had given Annie Oakley her first real prestige, was killed in his tent by Indian police before Buffalo Bill could reach him and induce him to surrender.

Buffalo Bill served under General Miles throughout the campaign which ended with the Battle of Wounded Knee. While at Standing Rock, N. D., he received some disconcerting news. It was that Annie Oakley was dead. Hastily he cabled England, where Miss Oakley and her husband had gone to fill some shooting engagements during the interim in which the members of the Buffalo Bill show wandered Europe without much knowledge of whether they ever again would appear with the "Scout of the Plains." Back came the answer:

232.

"Just finished big Christmas dinner, and feel fine. Mistake in name. Person who died was an opera singer."

Then Buffalo Bill did a typical thing. He hurried to a telegraph office and wrote a cable to London.

"Just received your message that you're all right. Awful glad. Aint you?"

When spring came again, Buffalo Bill was back with his show and touring Germany. It is rather a coincidence that this man, returned from a tiny war which ended with one battle, should give to another man ideas which would be used in the greatest war of all time. Wilhelm Hohenzollern was Emperor of Germany now. When the Buffalo Bill show came to this country, it afforded him a chance for study—but not concerning the history of the winning of America's West. It was an object lesson in the moving and feeding of armies.

The Kaiser's interest was renewed in the Buffalo Bill show and in the shooting of Annie Oakley when the aggregation started through Germany, and several performances were attended by him. This was followed by another private exhibition in which Frank Butler and Miss Oakley used some of their old rifle tricks,

233.

among them that of shooting the ashes from a
cigarette. This accomplished, the Kaiser showed
great interest in the trick, asked how it was performed, and then, with his almost mad enthusiasm for guns and shooting of all kinds, enquired
if Annie Oakley could repeat the feat with him
holding the target. Annie Oakley said she could
—and did. The ashes toppled from the cigarette, and a proud young ruler tucked away the
holder in which he had encased the tube of to-

*How "Little Sure Shot" might have prevented the
Great War. She is shown shooting the ash from
Kaiser Wilhelm's cigarette.*

234.

bacco, that he might save it for a souvenir. For years afterward, Annie Oakley congratulated herself on her good aim, and the fact that she hadn't missed her mark. Then suddenly she changed her mind and wished that she had. She even sat down, and in typical Annie Oakley style, wrote to the war mad monarch; stating her sorrow at having hit only a cigarette and asking for another shot. But the Kaiser did not reply. That, however, was in 1917. As for the war

plans made while the Buffalo Bill show toured
Germany:

"We saw the Kaiser five or six times during
our stay in Germany," says her diary, "His
thoughts were bent upon military efficiency to a
degree almost inconceivable to us at that time.
He did not care about the show as an exhibition,
but centered his entire interest upon the me-
chanical aspect of it and the lessons which could
be learned from us for use in the handling of his
military.

"We never moved without at least forty officers of the Prussian guard standing all about
with notebooks, taking down every detail of the
performance. They made minute notes of how
we pitched camp—the exact number of men
needed, every man's position, how long it took,
how we boarded the trains and packed the horses
and broke camp; every rope and bundle and kit
was inspected and mapped.

"But most of all, they took interest in our
kitchen. The traveling ranges were inspected
and enumerated in those endless notebooks. The
chefs were interviewed. The methods of storing
food, of preparing it, of having necessities ready
for use at a minute's notice, all these things were
jotted down. Naturally we were curious as to
why they were doing all this, and had our own

ideas about how it would be used in some way for the army—one could not travel in Germany even in those days without feeling sure that sooner or later the Kaiser would throw his nation into war. But we had no idea, of course, that the world was to listen, mouth open, twenty-five years later, to the stories of the marvelous traveling kitchens of the Teuton army, serving meals piping hot on the road to Brussel's—an idea gained from the Buffalo Bill Wild West show when we toured Germany!"

Two years more were left for Annie Oakley in Europe, a part of which time was consumed during a tour of Scotland with the show, and the rest being spent again at Earl's Court as an added attraction of the Horticultural Exhibit of 1892. Then back to American soil came the aggregation and the beginning of its present day reputation with its engagement as a part of the Chicago World's Fair in 1893. For then in truth did Colonel Cody's show become "Buffalo Bill's Wild West and Congress of Rough Riders of the World."

The show was a replete thing now of bolo throwers, cossacks, Arabs, and a collection of riders and exhibition artists from every part of the world. As for Annie Oakley, she was the same sensation at Chicago that she had been in

London and other parts of Europe. Incidentally, when the word "sensation" is used, it is not in the extravagant sense. To the ordinary mind, the work of the "Little Missy" was all but unbelievable. Her name became a household one in America; no political cartoon, it seemed, could reach the maximum without depicting some figure of the day in the dress of a girl marksman, shooting an apple from the head of a shivering adversary. Her name stood for everything in the world of rifledom. Stage burlesques featured "Annie Oakleaf" in comedy depictions of the Darke County girl. Guns were patterned for her; she added the trick of shooting glass balls while riding a bicycle and immediately every bicycle firm—cycling was then quite a fad in America—strove to inveigle her into using their product that they might advertise the fact that Annie Oakley deemed a certain make of cycle the only one to stand the terrific strain of the arena. The recognition of Annie Oakley upon the street meant that immediately a crowd would form, following in her wake, just to see the woman who had displayed her prowess before the royalty of Europe. Small boys screamed her name as they attended the Wild West; to them she was almost as much of a personage as that god of gods, Buffalo Bill. Outing garment houses copied her dresses. Annie Oakley was a fixture—or as much of a fixture as this country can possess—in the minds of the American populace.

For seven years after the World's Fair she continued to travel with the Buffalo Bill show, watching, incidentally, the processes which gradually led to its disintegration. There was, of course, the ending of the partnership between Nate Salsbury and Buffalo Bill and the beginning of a new one with James A. Bailey. The extravagant spending practised by the Colonel, the renting of entire floors of hotels, of the expenditure of money which he believed in his gullible way would continue to flow to him forever. And while he grew poorer, Annie Oakley and her husband, saving always, working in summer with the Wild West and in the winter at trap shooting events where inevitably they obtained not only a chance at the purses, but a share of the gate receipts as well, prepared for the day when they would need travel no more, and when there would be wealth sufficient to keep them always. At last they considered that this time had arrived, and consequently they made known their intention to end their days as an attraction with the Wild West show with the finish of the season of 1901.

ANNIE OAKLEY

The last performance was held. The band played its usual farewell music, "Auld Lang Syne." The show train was loaded and started upon its last journey of the season. Onward, onward through North Carolina it went, headed for the winter quarters—

A crash in the night. The screams of injured, the milling of animals, the rending of steel and wood, the hiss of escaping steam. The show train had met head-on with another, several persons had been killed and more than a hundred injured. Among them was Annie Oakley, pulled unconscious from the wreckage by her husband, and now, in the hospital, unconscious and wavering between life and death. All that night the balance was in doubt, while a watchful husband, stepping at intervals to the bedside of his unconscious wife, watched a strange transformation. The heavy chestnut hair was slowly changing. The next day, the doctors gave the verdict that Annie Oakley would live, but that she might never be able to move or shoot again. The Little Missy which the show world had known was gone. In her place was a mangled, elderly woman with white hair—hair which had been beautiful chestnut only seventeen hours before.

Five operations followed that accident, and years of agony. But the courage of Annie Oakley predominated always.   Two years later, a woman walked uncertainly to the traps of a gun club near Nutley, N. J. She fondled a shotgun, lifting it and lowering it, then gazing quizzically along its barrel.

"Pull!" she called, and a target flew forth. There was a lightning movement as a gun went to a feminine shoulder, a crackle of yellow blaze, and in the distance a splintered target. The white haired woman turned and smiled.

"Just as good as ever!" she remarked.

Annie Oakley had "come back."

Chapter Fourteen

IT was not as the hard riding, swift moving performer of the arena that Annie Oakley made her return to the shooting world. The injuries which she had sustained, with the consequent operations, had aged her to an extent almost unbelievable. However, she was determined; it was as though the accident had been a challenge to her. The retirement to which she had looked forward while with the Buffalo Bill show now seemed irksome and forced; by sheer strength of will and outdoor exercise, the woman rehabilitated herself to an extent where she again could ride with something of her old skill, while her shooting, under even heavier practise than formerly, even improved. Then the stage beckoned, and Annie Oakley acceded to the temptation. It was an unfortunate venture.

The play was "The Western Girl," and in the slang of today, it would be called "just one of those things." Miss Oakley's scrapbooks are not filled to overflowing with information concerning the opus. There is, however, a program

242.

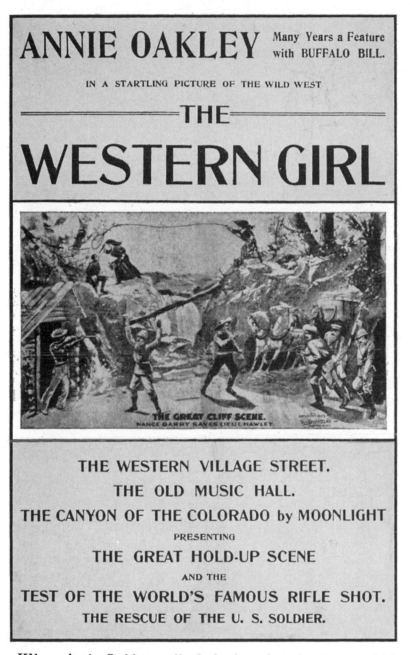

ANNIE OAKLEY Many Years a Feature
with BUFFALO BILL.

IN A STARTLING PICTURE OF THE WILD WEST

THE

WESTERN GIRL

THE GREAT CLIFF SCENE.
NANCE BARRY SAVES LIEUT. HAWLEY.

THE WESTERN VILLAGE STREET.
THE OLD MUSIC HALL.
THE CANYON OF THE COLORADO by MOONLIGHT
PRESENTING
THE GREAT HOLD-UP SCENE
AND THE
TEST OF THE WORLD'S FAMOUS RIFLE SHOT.
THE RESCUE OF THE U. S. SOLDIER.

When Annie Oakley walked the boards—the poster which heralded her later venture into "legitimate" drama.

which gives some light as to the quality of the production and what it counted upon to lure audiences:

ANNIE OAKLEY

in

THE WESTERN GIRL.

Synopsis:

"Act I—Village street in Fiddletown; the dead soldier; the half-breed has power; Lieutenant Hawley seeks revenge; Jim Barry and his blind daughter come to town; the half-breed attempts murder, and is stopped by Nance Barry, the sure shot. Mickey McGann has domestic troubles; the German scientist helps the poor, henpecked Irishman. The half-breed makes love to the blind girl, and ties her on his horse; the father interferes. We are partners in a gamble for money, but we are enemies when you gamble on the damnation of my daughter's soul. The half-breed calls for the Mexican girl, the gleam of a stiletto, the father is helpless; the half-breed makes a dash for liberty; the Western Girl proves the best rider and carries away the prize."

Please remember that this is only the first act, and as one can easily guess from the things she does, Nance Barry is the Western Girl, as played by Annie Oakley. So far, in one act, she has saved two lives, which was running a high average, even for the days when melodrama possessed more of interest than it does today. But to continue:

"Act II—Interior of the Mexican Music Hall. The Mexican girl dances for the boys; the half-breed shakes hands with Jim Barry. Mickey McGann is hunted down by his cyclone wife and is made to dance a two step home. Lieutenant Hawley fears trouble with the bandits and rides to Silver Creek for reinforcements. The Mexican girl bids him goodby with a curse. The German gets into a heap of trouble with the road agents, and plays a Yankee trick. The Western Girl seeks to help Lieutenant Hawley, but is held prisoner; the Mexican girl and the half-breed prove dangerous enemies. The Chinaman brings the washing. The lame fiddler plays a smart trick. The Western Girl fires a shot for liberty."

Thus the plot thickened in a work of art of which Annie Oakley said nothing in her notes, and saved but few reminders in her scrapbooks. To one who had performed before queens and kings, perhaps this effort, once she had found herself embroiled in its cast of characters, which, to judge from the Chinese, Mexican, Irish, German, Indian and other components, perhaps formed one of the originals for the League of Nations, was something better forgotten than cherished. But from a standpoint of humor,

ANNIE OAKLEY

The Western Girl was almost unforgettable. To wit, the third and fourth acts:

"Act III—Block House Canyon in the evening. Jim Barry, the king of bandits, intends to reform. Lieutenant Hawley is made captive; the arrival of the Silverwood coach; the holdup; the German has his baggage examined and the men marvel at the contents. The Irish lady is made to dance; the German again plays a Yankee trick. The quarrel among the men for a little mountain girl. Jim Barry plays a game of cards for his daughter's honor. I have lost my own soul. The Western Girl shoots at the heart of the one she loves; Hawley escapes, but is held to account by the Mexican girl. The bridge across the cliff has fallen; Nance Barry throws a lariat and the day is won for the Western Girl.

"Act IV—The Eagle's Nest in the mountains. The Western Girl shoots game; the two sisters are in love with one soldier; the father makes an awful mistake; the blind girl makes her life's sacrifice. The Irish lady has many tears and the German lends sympathy. The bandits demand the presence of their captain. The refusal; the gun at the heart of the blind girl; the timely arrival of Nance Barry; horses are galloping down the mountain. The Eagle's Nest will be destroyed, but the U. S. Cavalry and Lieutenant Hawley make a charge. The family is safe and the Eagle's Nest again a happy home. 'Love, love is a flower.' "

ANNIE OAKLEY

Evidently, the flower withered considerably. By April of 1903, Annie Oakley was away from the machinations of Mexicans and banditti, German, Chinese and Irish comedians, down in Darke County, Ohio, on a visit to her childhood haunts, where clear air could aid one in ridding the lungs of the acrid smoke of bandits' guns and the dusty charge of cavalry. Following this, she went back to the giving of exhibitions before gun clubs and the shooting of matches; wrecks, operations and even the experiences of being a Western Girl had not impaired her aim; soon sportsmen's magazines were carrying the stories that Annie Oakley was shooting with even better precision than she had known in the days when her white hair was chestnut colored and she was a favored star of the Buffalo Bill Wild West. But one morning she awoke in her home at Nutley, N. J., to learn how swiftly one may pass from public view, how completely even those who are supposed to know better can forget. It was perhaps the most grueling experience which Annie Oakley ever went through, for this carried more than physical torture; it was mental. Out of Chicago the wires of a press association had borne the following story:

246.

ANNIE OAKLEY

ANNIE OAKLEY ASKS COURT FOR MERCY

FAMOUS WOMAN CRACK-SHOT WHOM EDWARD VII APPLAUDED STEALS TO SECURE COCAINE.

"Annie Oakley, daughter-in-law of Buffalo Bill, and the most famous rifle shot in all the world, lies today in a cell at the Harrison Street station, under a bridewell sentence for stealing the trousers of a negro in order to get money with which to buy cocaine.

The woman for whose spectacular marksmanship King Edward himself once led the applause in the court yard of Buckingham Palace.

When arrested Saturday on the complaint of Charles Curtis, a negro, she was living at 140 Sherman Street. She gave the name of Elizabeth Cody, but it occurred to no one to connect her with Colonel Cody's famous daughter-in-law. Today, however, when brought before Justice Caverly, she admitted her guilt.

'I plead guilty, your honor, but I hope you will have pity upon me,' she begged. 'An uncontrollable appetite for drugs has brought me here. I began the use of it years ago to steady me under the strain of the life I was leading and now it has lost me everything. Please give me a chance to pull myself together.'

The striking beauty of the woman whom the crowds at the World's Fair admired is now entirely gone. Although she is but twenty-eight years old, she looks almost forty. Hers, in fact, is one of the extreme cases which have come up in the Harrison Street Police Court.

Today she will be taken to the bridewell to serve out a sentence of $45 and costs.

'A good stay in the bridewell will do you good,' said the court.

The prisoner's husband, Sam Cody, died in England. Their son Vivien, is now with Colonel Cody at the latter's ranch on the North Platte. The mother left "Buffalo Bill" two years ago, and has since been drifting around the country with stray shows."

Never, perhaps, was there a more deliberate slaughtering of the good name of a good woman. Nor was this all. Reporters who professed to have seen the Buffalo Bill show, and to have known Annie Oakley, interviewed the woman "Elizabeth Cody, daughter-in-law of Buffalo Bill" in her cell, and straightway went to their offices that they might write dilated accounts of the downfall of "Little Sure Shot." They told of her craving for cocaine, of her depths of despair, of the horror of her condition as a drug addict—and the real Annie Oakley read all this in her home at Nutley, N. J., with feelings impossible for her to describe.

All this is being told here for more reasons

than because of the part that it played in the life of Annie Oakley. For this "story" was more than a mere individual affair; it played its part in newspaper history, and did much to make news gathering agencies the more efficient human machines which they are today, and changed the aspects of a number of newspapers tremendously toward what makes news, and what should be considered before that news may be given to the public.

This was during a time of transition, when "yellow journalism" was at its height, having come into existence during the Spanish American war, and thrived upon the looseness of reports and so-called reports from the various seats of conflict. Rumors were often printed as facts, and too little thought was oft-times given to the fundamentals behind the news of the day and the effect that it might have upon those who prospered or suffered by it.

A woman, a drug addict, so it seems, had been arrested on the complaint of a negro at whose home she had been given shelter. She had stolen from him, and during the arraignment, according to the sifting of facts, a policeman noticed the name of Cody and made some joking remark about it, asking the woman if she were any relation to the renowned Buffalo Bill. She had answered in the affirmative. Then he had said:

"I suppose you're the woman who used to do all the shooting in the show."

The drug addict professed that she was the woman, and from that start the story of Annie Oakley's "downfall" had grown, a mass of fabrications, of loose reporting, looser editing and in fact, a general violation of all the rules by which reporters are supposed to give their gleanings to the public.

Annie Oakley's action was swift. The fighting instinct of Little Missy went to its highest pitch. Within a short time, more than fifty newspapers faced suits for libel in one of the greatest concerted actions ever brought. In all but two of the cases, Annie Oakley was successful, winning the suits and damages ranging from $500 to as high as $27,500, the last being against the main offender which had run "follow up stories," adding insult to injury. And that Annie Oakley was fighting mad may be gauged from her remarks to one of the juries which returned a verdict against her, if her notebooks are correct. For within them is a typewritten copy of a speech by which Annie Oakley vented her feelings:

In later years.

ANNIE OAKLEY

"Gentlemen of the Jury:

"You have measured the honor in which you hold the wives and daughters of your city by the verdict just rendered. To the defendants I would say, if the gentlemen who fought for this state during the Civil War conducted their defense with as much cowardice as the defense has been conducted against one lone little woman in this suit, I don't wonder that they were defeated. I will withdraw from the courtroom immediately, so as to give one or all of you gentlemen who are such gallant defenders of women's honor a chance to further your cowardice by shooting me in the back if you so choose!"

It has been said that these suits made newspaper history. They did more. They gave to newspapers a greater concern for investigation, and a lack of trustfulness which had been held before in the word of someone else. Today, in the average newspaper office, such a fabrication would be almost impossible, largely because of lessons taught years ago by the fighting spirit of a woman whose name, inadvertently and innocently in a number of cases where the facts were not at hand to prove or disprove the alleged facts of the dispatch, had been badly trampled in the dust.

Today, for instance, largely as a result of Annie Oakley's action and the necessity which it proved for careful checking of all accounts having to do with prominent persons, the reporter does not rush immediately to his office and write his story when someone gives him a "tip." Instead, he checks up on the information at the source, then, having armed himself with the alleged facts, goes to what is known as the "morgue" for comparisons.

Every newspaper is today equipped with a "morgue" of greater or lesser degree. In it are files of the newspaper since its inception, photographs of well-known persons, their complete life history, their antecedents and in fact, every possible fact connected with them. A visit to the "morgue" and a comparison would have shown, in the case of the Annie Oakley story:

First that Annie Oakley's name was not Cody, but Mrs. Frank E. Butler.

That her home was in Nutley, N. J., and that she had appeared in a professional role as late as a few weeks before.

That she had not been in Chicago since 1902.

That she had not been injured in Cincinnati, as was claimed by the drug addict, but that she had been ill for two years as the result of a railroad wreck in North Carolina.

That Buffalo Bill's only son, Kit Carson Cody, died when a baby in Rochester, New York.

That the woman who gave her age as twenty-eight could not be the real Annie Oakley since the date of birth of the genuine "Little Sure Shot" was 1860, fifteen years before the birth of the impostor.

That Annie Oakley—for pictures are kept up to date nowadays—and the impostor resembled each other in no particular.

And that, in the case of the slightest doubt, there must always be the interrogation on the part of the paper as to whether the person in question is or is not an impostor. It is no insult to a police character to infer that this character may be taking the name of a famous person in an effort to elicit sympathy. But it certainly is hard on a widely known person to announce that he or she is an habitue of police courts.

These safeguards have come to pass today. The comparison might be made of the lack of protection of human life which existed upon railroads of a quarter of a century ago and those which conform to the United States Safety Appliances in use today. Accidents made the railroads better. The Annie Oakley accident made newspapers, many of which were suffering innocently from yellow journalism, better, not only for the readers, but for themselves and those concerning whom they published news. It is interesting, incidentally, to note from the reports of the various trials, that Annie Oakley did not embroil herself in a fight with the newspapers of America. Instead, she was aided by numerous dailies; some of which were those which had fallen an innocent victim to the story and did their best to show their sincerity of amends by doing everything in their power to make such an occurrence impossible in the future. And that at least one of the offending papers, not only forgave her anger but condoned it, is exhibited in an old scrapbook, found in the effects of the markswoman. The letter accompanied a piece of extremely favorable publicity and read:

Hoboken, N. J.

Dear Mrs. Butler:

Although you dug into us for three thousand "Iron Men" at a time when three thousand was a large sum with us—you see we still love you.

Yours very truly,

The Hudson Observer.

Chapter Fifteen

THERE was still another angle to the newspaper tangle, and that was the proof which it gave to the unimpeachable character of a woman who had proved by her actions and by her accomplishments that the results of a lifetime are the responsibility of the one who lives it, and not, as is so often claimed, the result of the surroundings into which one is thrown. Annie Oakley, in the opinion of many persons, eternally damned herself when she became the wife of an actor. But the investigations attendant upon the Chicago incident proved conclusively otherwise.

One defendant chose to fight with every possible weapon, believing that a person who had led the wandering life of an actress in variety, the sole white woman with an aggregation of cowboys and vaqueros and western characters, a circus woman, easily could be proved to be a loose, dissolute sort of human, and that the court action could be nullified by counter claims and accusations. It therefore raised a pool for the purpose of investigation, hired detectives, pried into every angle of the life of Annie Oakley and

strove mightily for even a few grains of conso-
lation in the discovery of untoward actions.

Naturally, it is the failing of a biographer to
exalt his character. All too often, a person
under favorable observation, becomes a paragon
of virtue, traits of character that are not con-
ducive to good reading or to pedestal deserving
qualities are overlooked. But in the case of
Annie Oakley, this biographer finds himself in
the position of the investigators who worked so
indefatigably a quarter of a century ago. For
their sole findings were that Annie Oakley was
a determined little, white haired woman who
since her childhood had adhered strictly in the
main elements of life to the Quaker teachings of
her mother. They found that one of her favorite bits of reading matter was the Bible, and
that between shows and in periods of rest, this
book was the one which formed her chief solace
and diversion. They found that among the entire Wild West, every cowboy, every working-
man was not only ready but eager to fight for the
honor of a woman who, in seventeen years with
the show, never had done an illicit thing. That,
unostentatiously, hiding her actions in a queer,
stolid form of modesty, she conducted her own
charities, providing for whole families, and
sending girl after girl who otherwise could not

256.

afford it, to school, that they might escape the longings for education which she had possessed. Scratch and dig, investigate and furrow, neither those investigators nor this biographer have been able to discover in the life of Annie Oakley anything save an almost incomprehensible collection of virtues; one finds himself wondering if the woman could have been real, if after all she were not the fiction character which her life seemed to make her. Quiet, modest, honorable; faithful to the man who was so thoroughly faithful to her—for one finds Frank Butler still writing poetry after the hair had turned white and the world seemed less roseate than in the days when the Prince of Wales applauded Little Sure Shot —considerate, kindly, generous, gentle, yet with a will as firm and as unbendable as tungsten steel; these are the attributes which one must give to Annie Oakley when perhaps better reading might be vended had she been a George Sand or a rifle-wielding Lucrezia Borgia.

Annie Oakley did not take advantage of her new flare of publicity, even though many newspapers, in their anxiety to make amends for a regrettable incident in which they had played the part of the innocent bystander, would have been more than willing for the opportunity to repay her by effulgent publicity of a favorable character. Instead, with her husband, she continued her appearances at the various shoots, and for a time gave exhibitions at gun clubs where the clientele was strictly concerned with the sportsman element and where most of the publicity came from papers which had figured not at all in the Chicago fiasco. This continued for a number of years. Then came again the yearning to return to the arena.

However, conditions were not what they had been in former times. The Buffalo Bill show, for instance, after many difficulties, had become the Buffalo Bill Wild West and Pawnee Bill's Far East, fighting against the debts which had accrued in the past before the advent of Pawnee Bill, and doomed to close its doors forever a year later in Denver when Buffalo Bill ceased to be a figure at the head of his organization and became an individual feature with the Sells Floto Circus. Annie Oakley's engagement this time —it was 1912—was with the Young Buffalo Wild West, a fair imitation of the real Buffalo Bill show. However, there was not the zest of old. For one thing, the show was not the dashing, tremendous organization with which she once had formed such an important figure. Then too, the years had taken their toll; Annie Oakley was more than fifty now; that, combined with

258.

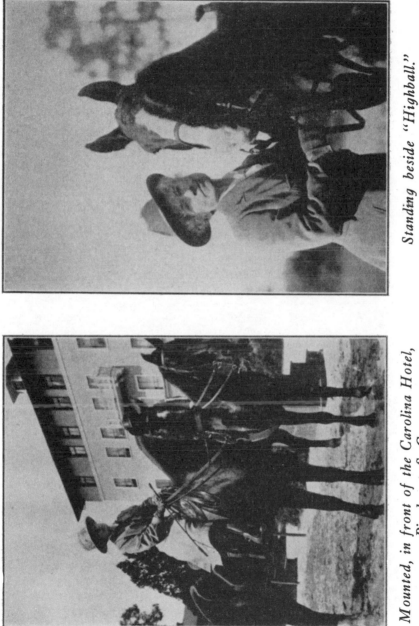

Standing beside "Highball."

Mounted, in front of the Carolina Hotel,
Pinehurst, S. C.

the aging influence of her accident made show life far from the agreeable thing which it had been in other years. Consequently at the end of her contract, she retired from the show world forever, and in 1916 took the position as a teacher of gunship for women at the fashionable resort of Pinehurst, N. C.

Here, for two years, was the ideal life. There were her horses and her dogs, the pleasant duties of "professor" at the traps or before the target, sallies after quail, rest and quiet, with now and then a professional match thrown in, at which Annie Oakley, in spite of the years which had departed, still displayed the old prowess, the old keenness of action and of sight. A clipping is before this writer. It is dated February 1916 and reads:

"Annie Oakley delighted 800 persons and proved that she had lost none of her skill with firearms in an exhibition at Pinehurst, N. C., recently. With a rifle, she hit coins tossed in the air and broke marbles on the fly; she shot a cigarette from the hand of her husband, Frank Butler, and an apple from the head of her setter, Dave. With a revolver, she rolled a tin can along the ground with a tattoo of bullets on its upper crust and exploded cartridges thrown into the air. She broke a ball whirled about a man's head while she sighted by looking into the mirror formed by the blade of a table knife. With a shotgun, Mrs. Butler proved her speed. Mr. Butler threw six balls into the air simultaneously. The woman expert, using three double barrelled shotguns, broke them all before they struck the ground."

Nor was that all; a year later, at the Wentworth Gun Club, New Hampshire, she broke the club's record of 97 hits, by a perfect score of 100 straight targets. This, if you please, at fifty-eight; a white haired woman once condemned to die and saved only by five operations.

Perhaps the time spent at Pinehurst was the happiest of Annie Oakley's later life. In spite of the fact that more than three thousand five hundred women came to her as novices, only to depart skilled in the use of firearms, there was plenty of time for rest and for recreation and retrospect. Time too for wandering the hills and dales, for riding and for hunting, for training her dogs, of which Dave, the amiable setter, formed the most beloved, followed closely by Fred, named for Fred Stone, the actor, as was her favorite horse. Time for memories, as is indicated by a clipping and a letter.

The clipping was from the Conning Tower of the New York Tribune, cherished in Annie Oakley's collection:

"Advice from Pinehurst, N. C., is to the effect that Annie Oakley is down there giving instruction

ANNIE OAKLEY

daily from 11 to 12, in the art of shooting. 'Here she is,' writes H. A. W., 'a white-haired, picturesque feature at Pinehurst, teaching all the ladies to break glass balls with a rifle, or clay pigeons with a shotgun. No longer a short-skirted, dashing girl of the plains, but a nice little old lady with spectacles and knitting. Only one thing remains—her 100 per cent ability to break glass balls.' "

To which the Conning Tower conductor had added:

"And in 1893 Annie Oakley who shot glass balls with far greater precision than Colonel Cody used to shoot them, was one of the few women we really loved. And now all the new generation knows of Annie Oakley is that she is in the hodiernal slang."

Annie Oakley wrote a letter to the Conning Tower in answer to that statement; evidently a letter which gave her pleasure, for she saved a carbon copy of it, pasted side by side with the clipping. It was a missive of retrospection, of happiness in things long gone. And it is too an excellent insight into the character of the woman whom other generations knew as "Little Sure Shot":

Pinehurst, N. C., February 2, 1917.
"My dear Mr. Conning Tower Man:
"What did I hear you say? She is a little, white haired lady who wears spectacles and knits? I am

guilty as to the first two charges owing to two trains which tried to pass on the same track but did not succeed. My hair turned white in seventeen hours from the injuries received, and the result was five operations. That was in 1901, and in 1911, blood poison caused by infection from a slight operation resulted in four days with a temperature of one hundred and seven which affected my right eye so that sight was impaired for reading fine print or doing fancy work of which I am very fond.

"Not guilty as to knitting. I graduated from the knitting school at the age of eight years. That was when I started to shoot. Since then, I have not handled the knitting needles. So your friend Mr. White could not see at close range when he mistook the embroidering for knitting.

"Why did I give up the arena? Because I made hay in the hay-day of my youth and felt that I had earned a change. Why am I teaching ladies to shoot? Well, that is my pleasure, for which there is no charge or compensation on my part. What else do I do? Go out after Mr. Reynard once a week, and with the assistance of Fred, my bronco, after a fifteen or sometimes twenty mile chase, we bring Mr. Fox's scalp back to Pinehurst, where my husband and I make our winter home, or arise with the sun and hie me off into the woods or fields with my beautiful dog, Dave, in quest of quail. A twelve or fifteen mile trip makes me sleep and dream again of the days when I ran bare-footed over hill and dale, chasing the bees and butterflies or climbing nimbly up a dogwood tree to pick the finest of blossoms to weave in a real queen's crown with the gorgeous wild roses festooned from my head to my then little pink toes. How I loved the call of the woods with their wealth of wild flowers, the hum of the bees, the sweet notes of the turtle dove; the drumming of the ruffled grouse and the call of the Bob-white. It was a haven of peace to sit on the old, moss covered logs and inhale the scent of the tall ferns.

"Then, at sunset, a sweet faced, white capped little mother, who watched, smiling, the homecoming of her one little tomboy of the family. The sweet days of childhood are long past, and the dear mother sleeps at the little resting place close by.

"Then the great fight for recognition in the arena. It was uphill work, for when I began there was a prejudice to live down, but thanks to many of our good, American people, they gave me generously, both of their approval and their applause, and so I am rather proud of your compliment in the Tribune of January 11:

" 'She was one of the few women we really loved.'

"Thank you, Mr. Conning Tower Man, and may you give some encouraging message to others who are just beginning the great battle of life.

"Very truly yours
"Annie Oakley."

But the dream days, and the roving days at Pinehurst, when Annie Oakley—imaginative as she always was—lived again the times of a childhood, came to an end as the result of an action by

ANNIE OAKLEY

a man whom she once had met and whom a miss
in aim would have removed from the earth—
Kaiser Wilhelm of Germany. War came to
America, and with it a militant spirit arose in
the breast of the crackshot. At first she surged
with the ambitious idea of raising a regiment
of women from those she had taught to be expert
marksmen, but with the application of her common sense to the thought, it died. But there was
something she could do, she and Frank and
Dave, and she set about it forthwith. That was
to make life a bit lighter for the men in camp,
to aid with the raising of funds and the setting
of an example in the art of hitting the enemy before he hit you.

Consequently, with Mr. Butler and the amiable setter, Dave, the three set forth upon a
gratuitous tour of the army camps. Money for
their services was refused, likewise reimburse-
ment for expenses. It was Annie Oakley's way
of doing her part in the great war and there
could be no return for it.

At camp after camp they shot, Frank Butler
and Annie Oakley doing their various feats. All
this while old Dave, a lop eared, genial appearing setter, took a role that had already played
an important part in the lives of the two crack-
shots—Dave, for the purposes of entertaining

264.

soldiers, stepped into the place left vacant by George, long ago. Now, grinning, his tongue lolling, his tail wagging ever so slightly lest a stronger motion might displace the target, it was Dave who sat with the apple on his head, waiting for his William Tell mistress to knock it off with a shot from her rifle. Nor was it long until Dave did more than fill the role of an ordinary performer. He became a money getter for the Red Cross.

There came the necessity for odd ways of raising funds; money was not coming as fast as the demands called for. Then it was that Dave— he became Captain Dave of the Red Cross shortly afterward—stepped into the breach. Together Frank Butler and Annie Oakley taught him the trick. Then spectators at the various events were asked to allow Dave to scent a handkerchief. After that, Dave was taken away, where he could not watch what followed. An amount of money—whatever the participant desired to risk on the trial—was placed in the handkerchief and the bit of linen hidden anywhere the donor chose within a distance of 100 yards. Then, Dave was turned loose, with the agreement that, providing he found the money, it was to go to the Red Cross, and if he failed, the other partner in the game was to receive credit for having offered it. But not in one instance did Dave fail.

The old setter would leap from his captors and make a short circle of the enclosure. Then with his nose to the ground, he would strike the trail, following it surely and quickly to the hiding place, there to dislodge it, and with wagging tail await the arrival of the Red Cross officer to take charge of it. In this manner, in the vicinity of Portsmouth, N. H. alone, old Dave raised $1625 for the benefit of the men in France.

So went the war work, followed through until the signing of the armistice. Then again, the exhibitions, fewer in number now. The increasing rest was earned; at Pinehurst, some time previous, she had met one of the physicians who had attended her shortly after the wreck of the Buffalo Bill Wild West at which time the prediction had been made that she never would shoot again. Their conversation brought forth the fact that since the edict, Annie Oakley had participated in 1,407 shooting events and exhibitions, during which time she had broken the records of a number of gun clubs.

After the war, however, there was little of the old work of matches and stakes; Annie Oakley and her husband felt that they had garnered enough of worldly wealth; henceforth their

266.

"Dave"—canine son of William Tell. He did his bit in the war by allowing his mistress to shatter thousands of apples from his head.

main work would be exhibitions for the purposes of charity. In this connection, she shot before her last great crowd at the show held by Fred Stone at his place at Mineola, L. I. for the benefit of the Occupation Therapy Society of New York, an organization devoted to the rehabilitation of war veterans. Several other lesser exhibitions followed, and then, in November, near Daytona, Fla., an automobile in which Annie Oakley was riding, turned turtle while speeding along a Florida road. This time, the doctors said that her fate was sealed.

Sixty-two years old; a hip fractured, the tendons of her right leg pulled so badly as to necessitate the steel support of a brace—these were the barricades which raised themselves between the Little Missy and the crack of a gun which she loved so well. She would never shoot again, they said.

"But they've said that before," answered Annie Oakley. "I've been near death four times in my life and the Good Lord has always pulled me through. He'll pull me through this time too. I'll shoot again, and I'll be as good as ever."

When the spring training season began for the ball clubs the next year, an automobile rolled slowly out to Cooke Field at Leesburg, Fla., containing a gentle, smiling man who lifted a broken wisp of a woman from the tonneau and steadying her, adjusted her crutches. She moved slowly, painfully toward a table near the grandstand where some guns awaited; this place had been selected because of friendship and because of its comparative seclusion save for those who knew the man and woman and who would sympathize if she failed.

Slowly, crutch-step after crutch-step, she covered the distance; frail, silvery haired, her face lined by suffering. A look of apprehension was in her eyes, almost of fear. Then slowly a thin hand left its crutch handle and reaching forward, touched a gun. A smile came to the aged lips. Annie Oakley turned.

"You know," she said in her quiet voice, "I haven't had a gun in my hand since the eighth of last October. I don't know—."

Across the field, a group of negro boys, worshippers of ball-players, had gathered, watching this little old lady who wanted to shoot. Slowly she steadied herself on her left foot so that it bore the burden of her body, and allowed her crutches to fall. She raised a rifle, slowly, carefully.

"All right!" she ordered, and a penny flew into the air. There was the crackle of a rifle, the sharp ping-g-g-g-g-g of contact, and the coin,

268.

dented by a bullet, flew glittering over the field to fall at last among the tumbling forms of the black boys, scrambling for the souvenir. Time after time was the performance repeated, until twenty-five straight hits had been recorded. Then disks of a larger size were thrown at a greater distance, Annie Oakley hit those too. Finally, with her left hand, still steadying herself upon that one foot, she tossed five eggs into the air at once and got them all before they could strike the ground. Proudly, the elderly woman turned and put forth her hands for her crutches.

"I knew I would be able to shoot again!" she said.

Nor was it the last time. Gradually she improved until she could dispense with the crutches, her main support being a steel brace about her right leg.

And as she improved in strength, she improved also in her shooting, with the result that eighteen months after her accident, she broke the club record of the Mayview Manor gun club at Blowing Rock, with a score of 98 out of a possible 100 targets while shooting at clay pigeons.

But finally the exhibitions dwindled. Gradually too, there began to flow to Annie Oakley, now living in Dayton, Ohio, near the scenes she had known in childhood, letters of cheer from those who knew her well. Word spread to her sister, Huldie Haines, to her brother, John Mozee of far off Oklahoma, and to her friendly niece, Fern Campbell of Detroit, that she was facing her last target. Gradually the news passed around, among the stars of the theater who had known and loved this woman for years —Will Rogers, Fred and Allene Stone and their daughter Dorothy of *Stepping Stones* fame, and others, that a visit to Dayton must not be complete without a visit to a modest home where a white haired woman, now becoming more and more of an invalid as the result of her Florida accident, strove to fight pain and loneliness and the knowledge that the woods and dales, the clearness of open sky and the haze of the stubble field were denied her forever. And at last there traveled forth the dispatch that Annie Oakley was dead. A little later—later by less than a single turn of the moon—her side partner, Frank Butler, followed to the grave.

The mention of rifles and Buffalo Bill and other romantic things caused more than one boy to read carefully that notice of Annie Oakley's death. It caused too a question which would never have been thought of, thirty years ago. But today:

"Pop; who was Annie Oakley?" came the query in many a home when the short dispatch made known the fact that the "Little Missy" was gone. And in many a home, an interrogated father halted in his reading. The room had faded. In its place, a great ampitheater stretched in a vastness of distance, of flying forms, of scenery, of throng-packed tiers of seats. At one side there waved and nodded the eagle-plumed headdresses of the representatives of the Sioux, the Kiowa, the Comanche and the Cheyenne. Yonder a stalwart man in flowing hair and straight brushed goatee, his buckskin coat fitting snug over massive shoulders, rode like a god upon his prancing horse. Farther away, the old Deadwood Stagecoach awaited the cue for the daily encounter with the "deadly aborigine of mountain and plain." And right out there— less than a score of feet away, shooting against Johnny Baker for the "champeenship" of the Wild West—

"Who was Annie Oakley?" asked many a father that night. "She was my first sweetheart, Son."

THE END